D'TURMAN TO SURVIVE

Based on a true story
Marked for Death by the
Milwaukee Cannibal,
Jeffrey Dahmer

JEROME TURMAN

PAGE PUBLISHING
Conneaut Lake, PA

First originally published by Page Publishing 2024

ISBN 979-8-89157-599-8 (pbk)
ISBN 979-8-89553-005-4 (hc)
ISBN 979-8-89157-641-4 (digital)

Author's Note

This book is based on a true story. Some names have been changed to protect the privacy of those involved, and some events have been modified for legal and dramatic purposes.

Content Warning: Graphic depictions of violence and murder.

CHAPTER 1

A Monster Among Us

The light of the television illuminates the dark room. On the screen, the movie *Star Wars: Return of the Jedi* is playing.

"I love this movie. The Emperor is my favorite character," he says. "Do you like movies?"

He glances back toward the boy in the corner. The boy struggles to overcome the chemical restraints of the toxic drug triazolam that is overtaking his system. He starts muttering incoherently. The boy's eyes are wide with fear and terror.

He shrugs. "I guess we're all entitled to our own opinions."

He stands up with intent and goes over to him. The young man appears to be around the age of sixteen or seventeen. He scoots away as far as he could, feeling threatened as to what may happen next, to no avail. He watches as the toxicity in the boy's body finally leaves him debilitated and in a vulnerable state of paralysis.

Dahmer straddles his weakened victim with satisfaction, slowly places his hands around his suitor's neck, and starts to squeeze with great intensity, restricting the airflow in the trachea. Dahmer starts to drift off into a delusional fantasy while slowly squeezing the life out of the helpless boy. After the boy slips into unconsciousness, Dahmer continues to apply pressure and cut off all forms of oxygen to the boy's brain until his lifeless body lies motionless on his living room floor. After a feeling of euphoria, Dahmer releases his hands and stands over his latest victim. He stares at the dead body before him and admires his work.

After a moment of inspiration and admiring the empty, soulless body, he walks over to his dresser, grabs a camera, and starts to take pictures of the boy. He poses the body in various suggestive positions trying to relive the event that he just instigated and carried out to the bitter end.

After staging the crime scene to mirror his sick fantasies, Dahmer realizes that he now has a human body that must be disposed of. Dahmer premeditates a well-thought-out and cleverly organized plan. He has prepared for this next phase. He pulls out a large hunting knife and rubber gloves and proceeds to dismember the body. He slits the body from the sternum to the lower belly and removes the internal organs. He then cuts the flesh off his legs and calves and up his left side, after removing each part of the empty human shell by picking it apart piece by piece, until he finally reaches the head.

He takes a great painstaking effort to carefully remove it because he has disturbing plans for this repulsive prize possession. He wants to keep it as a trophy. To hold it and talk to it and relive the time they spent together and the gruesome murder over and over again.

Eventually, he knows the head would start to decay, and that's not what Dahmer wanted. So he delicately peels off the skin from the skull, takes the head, and boils it to remove all reminiscent of the dead flesh. The end result is a clean and pristine bare-boned skull that he can admire and reminisce and relive his fantasies of this night.

After restarting the paused movie, Dahmer realizes that it has reached the climax of the film. The room now smells of freshly cooked meat coming from the kitchen.

"This is my favorite part," he says to himself and the skull that is propped up on the worn sofa next to him. His legs are propped up on the coffee table, and a knife, and the pictures displayed before him.

He sinks lower onto the couch and watches the rest of the movie, licking his bloodstained hands clean.[1]

---

[1] Davis, Donald A. November 15, 1991. *The Jeffrey Dahmer Story*. St. Martin's Paperbacks.

CHAPTER 2

Taxi Driver

I am standing alone, center stage, on a large, elevated platform at one of Milwaukee's many summer festivals dressed in a red leather jacket with numerous zippers, tight black leather pants, glowing white socks, and one large sequence glove on my right hand. I can feel the sweat starting to bead up across my forehead as dozens of bright lights shine directly on me.

Excitement and adrenaline flow through my body as I stand perfectly still before grabbing the black fedora hanging on the microphone. I slowly place it over the top of my head, turn to my right side, and pose. My right hand holds the fedora close to my head, and my right leg is bent at the knee with my toes pointed downward and just slightly lifted off the ground.

Thousands of screaming fans are cheering for me to start the show. I hear the music start to vibrate from the speakers. The bass is pounding, and the drums are beating to a chorus of rhythmic beats. I start to move, and the fans go wild! I can barely hear the music over their screams of ecstasy. My performance starts out slow and gentle before increasing in speed and excitement until it becomes a beautifully choreographed dance routine.

An hour and several songs later, the show comes to an end. My night as a Michael Jackson impersonator is over. My legs feel like cinder blocks, and my breathing is heavy as I walk off the stage and over to my cousin Harry.

"You killed it out there today, J," Harry says, clapping me on the back.

I wince then give him a tired smile. "Thanks, Harry, now it's time to get home and go to bed."

"Go to bed? My man, it's the middle of the afternoon."

"You think that's going to stop me?"

We both laugh as Harry walks over to a pay phone and calls us a cab.

We mingle with the fans for a little while until the cab finally pulls up. Waving goodbye, we head out. While Harry gives the driver our destination, I close my eyes and drift off.

While I am out, my cousin starts noticing the taxi driver keeps glancing back at us through his rearview mirror. Scowling, Harry keeps his gaze toward the passenger window, using the outside world as a distraction from the creep in the front seat. That's when he realizes the streets we pass are not any that he recognizes.

"Yo, where are we going?" Harry asks.

He turns his gaze forward to find the cab driver looking directly at Harry through the rearview mirror.

"Where are we going?" Harry repeats.

The cab driver doesn't say a word.

Harry pursed his lips. "We live on the Northside of town, and this doesn't look like the Northside to me. I don't think we're going in the right direction…sir."

The cab driver focuses his attention back on the road.

"I'll get you home," the driver says. "I'm just trying to avoid downtown traffic."

He turns his head to glance back at Harry, just enough for Harry to get a good look at his dark-brown eyes.

Harry quickly looks back toward the passenger window as he tries to calm his racing heart. He stares at every street sign they pass, desperately hoping to see one he recognizes all the while he can feel the gaze of the driver on him through the rearview mirror.

When he can't take it anymore, Harry shakes me awake. I blink in surprise and rub my eyes. "Are we home yet?"

Harry doesn't respond.

"Harry?"

I turn and follow his gaze out the window. Outside I see us pass a familiar McDonald's located just a few blocks from our house.

Harry lets out a deep sigh. "Yeah," he says. "Almost."

CHAPTER 3

Shoot To Kill

When he pulls up to our house, I look forward to the driver. "How much?" I ask.

He lifts his head and shifts his eyes toward the rearview mirror. "Sixty bucks."

I nod my head in approval as I pull out my wallet and grab three twenty-dollar bills.

"Do you have ten dollars for a tip?" I ask my cousin.

Harry shrugs his shoulders and then digs in his pocket before pulling out a five-dollar bill. "This is all I have."

I sigh and shake my head. "Never mind, I got it." I pull out another twenty-dollar bill from my wallet and give the money to the driver.

He takes the money and only then pushes a button unlocking the back doors. Harry and I step out of the cab and walk up to the driveway and toward the front door, stopping to wave goodbye to the taxi driver still parked across the street from our house before unlocking the front door, entering the house, and closing the door behind us.

My mom and dad are sitting in the living room watching TV when we walk in.

"Honey," my mother said, "you have a visitor."

I look down the hall and see my girlfriend, Lisa, walking out of the bathroom. Without a second's hesitation, she runs down the hall and wraps me in her arms, pulling me into an embrace.

"Hi, baby," she says in my ear.

I looked into her eyes, the eyes that, even after two years, I never get tired of. We have been dating since high-school.

"What are you doing here?" I ask her, returning her embrace. "You didn't tell me you were coming by."

"I wanted to surprise you." Lisa pulls away from me, her hands rubbing my arms as she looks up at me. "Aren't you happy to see me?"

I grab her hand and interlock her fingers with mine. "Of course I am," I say as I lean down and kiss her forehead.

It's not like I'm not happy to see her, but I am exhausted. In truth, I just want to go to bed and take a long nap, but I know that isn't going to happen anytime soon now.

I smile at Lisa, take her by the hand, and lead her to the adjacent rec room so we can hang out and watch a movie, just like she likes to do.

"Harry dear, did you lock the door?"

"I'm sure I did, Aunt Ruby," Harry says as he walks into the living room.

"Please double-check, honey."

"Okay, Auntie."

Harry begrudgingly walks to the front door and checks. It is locked just as he says. As he turns to walk away, he glances at the window, and what he sees outside causes him to do a double take. He stands there frozen as the color begins to drain from his face.

"He's still here," he says.

"Who's here?" Ruby asks.

"The cab driver." Harry quickly shut the blinds. "He's still sitting outside the house."

Ruby furrows her eyes. "Did you pay him?"

"Yeah, we gave him sixty bucks and a twenty-dollar tip."

Ruby stands up from the sofa and walks over to peek out of the blinds. "I'm sure he's just looking at his map to try and figure out how to reach his next destination." She closes the blinds once more and heads back toward the couch. "Give him time. He'll be gone in a few minutes."

With a huff, Harry goes to sit down next to his aunt, hoping some TV will ease his mind.

About thirty minutes later, Harry almost forgets about the taxi driver. But just to be safe, he decides to take a look outside anyway. Getting up from the couch and walking over to the front door, he lifts his head to look out of the small window at the top of the door.

He is met with two dark-brown eyes staring back at him.

Harry jumps back with a shout, pulling the attention of everyone else in the room.

The taxi driver is standing on the front porch perfectly still, his hood up and a backpack slung over his shoulder, his teeth clenched so tightly they look as if they may shatter at any moment.

"H-He's still here!" Harry shouts, pointing at the door. "He's standing on our doorstep!"

For the first time, my father, Frank, takes an interest in the situation. He stands up and walks over to the closed front door and looks out of the window.

There's no one there.

Frank opens the door, walks outside, and looks around. "Harry, what are you talking about?" he says, walking back into the house. "There's no one out there."

"I'm telling you, Uncle Frankie, he was standing right there!" Harry says, his voice several octaves higher than normal.

"Well, he's gone now." Frank closes the door. "Harry, you're seeing things. Let it go," says Frank.

"But he—"

"I said let it go." Frank walks away, sits back down, and continues to watch television.

Shaken up by what he has seen, Harry immediately rushes to the rec room where Lisa and I are watching a movie.

"J, I got to talk to you!" Harry says.

"What's up?" I ask, pausing the movie.

"That taxi driver? He was standing at our front door!"

"For real? No way."

Harry nods frantically. "I know what I saw. I looked right at him! He didn't seem right."

"So what happened?" Lisa asks, clearly more invested in the house drama than she was in the movie. "Where is he now?"

"Uncle Frankie went outside to look, but he had left by then."

"Creepy," Lisa says.

"What matters is that he's finally gone," I say, unpausing the movie.

"Do you think he'll come back?" Lisa asks us both.

"Doubtful," I say.

"I hope not," Harry confesses.

There's a hard knock at the front door.

We all look at each other before slowly walking out of the rec room and into the living room. My dad is standing at the front door looking out of the window. His ordinarily stoic expression is distorted. His jaw is locked in place, his eyes piercing with anger, and his face is flush.

I take a step closer. "What's wrong, Dad?"

Frank looks at my mother. "Get my guns."

Ruby slowly stands to her feet. "Frankie? What's going on?"

"Get my guns, now!"

With a sharp intake of breath, Ruby rushes toward the master bedroom.

Harry, Lisa, and I stand there, frozen in place. Lisa looks at me and mouths the word "Guns?" I shake my head and shrug my arms.

Harry is the first of us to muster up the courage to speak. He clears his throat. "Is…is he back?"

The look in my father's eyes tells us all that we need to know.

Frank walks past us and looks down the hall. "Ruby!" he shouts. "The guns!"

My mom rushes back into the living room carrying two rifles and a shotgun I don't even know we own. "Frankie," Ruby says. "Let's not be irrational."

"There ain't nothing irrational about protecting my family."

"You can't just go out there and shoot that man!"

Frank takes the guns from Ruby's hands and calls Harry and me to come over to him.

"You two go and man each door of the house," he says to us as he shoves the guns into our hands. "If he tries to come in, blow him away."

I stare at the weapon in my hand. The weight of what's happening is finally beginning to sink in. "Dad," I say. "I'm not shooting anybody."

My gaze is forced away from the gun and up to my father's eyes as he roughly presses his forehead against mine. "Boy," he begins. "You better take this rifle and do what I tell you to do, you hear?"

I stay silent.

"Do you hear me!" Frank says louder.

"Yes, sir," I finally muster.

"Then go!"

I do what I am told, worried at that moment that if I don't, his gun's barrel may end up pointed at me instead.

"I'm calling the police," Ruby says.

"Do what you want," Frank says. He cocks the shotgun in his hand. "But this will be over before they get here."

"M-Maybe we should try to talk to him and see what he wants?" Lisa says, trying to deescalate the situation.

"I asked him what he wanted through the door, but he just looked at me and walked away," says Frank.

"Maybe he didn't hear you?"

"He heard me. I know he did. His smile before walking away told me everything I needed to know." Frank takes his place at the front door, shotgun at the ready. "If he walks up to my door again, they'll be the last steps he ever takes."

Lisa takes a few steps back then turns to look at me while I'm standing and pointing my gun at the back door. Her expression is one of genuine fear, and I can only respond with a look that mirrors her own.

The gun shakes in my hand. I start to pray frantically, "Father in heaven, please, I beg of You, help me! I'm scared of what I may have to do. Deliver me from this evil predicament. This strange man prowling outside our home may wish to hurt us. I have no desire to harm this man, but I can't let him break in and assault my family. I don't know what to do. Please don't let me have to use this gun, and please don't let my home become my tomb. Evil stands at the door awaiting our downfall while the instrument of death clings to my trembling hands. My heart is racing fast as though it were running a marathon. I feel frozen in time and yet time won't stop. I don't want to do this. Please don't make me do this. I desperately need a perfect solution to this problem, Your perfect solution. Here I am, O Lord, please take my hand as I am drowning in my tears of fear."

I start to gasp for air, my spirit withers within me, my body trembles with sweat, and then suddenly, I remember the words of the Lord from Matthew 7: "Ask and it shall be given unto you. Seek and ye shall find. Knock and the door shall be opened unto you."

I close my tear-filled eyes as I begin to pray once more, "Here I am, O Lord, I seek You, and I ask You for Your help. I am trusting that my petition comes before you in your Holy temple. I beg of Thee, please be my salvation, for I have no desire to shed blood. The danger lurks just outside my door. I'm trusting you to direct the devil away from my home and to send evil down another path. For I am powerless to change or alter this situation, but You have all power and You can change the direction of this circumstance. For nothing can stand between Your love and protection of those who trust in You. So I am leaning on you and standing before Your throne and knocking. Please, dear Lord, open a door of escape."

I find myself turning my gaze away from the locked door before me and focusing my eyes on my cousin, who is standing at his post wielding a gun awaiting the moment of truth, just like me. I hear my mother's cry, pleading with my father to stop this madness. If only she can get through to him.

"Deliver us, O Lord," I pray. "From this suffocating anxiety of shedding blood that has overcome me and the people that I love. We have no desire to kill, but we are not yet ready to die. Please have mercy on us. Let Your will be done. But if it is not Your will that I should live or that others may die, give me the strength and the wisdom to do whatever is pleasing and acceptable to You, that I sin not against You. In Jesus's name, I pray. Amen."

I lift my eyes back toward the locked door in front of me and wait for an answer. I suddenly hear my mother screaming on the phone.

"Please help! Please help!" Ruby says when she finally reaches the police station. "Someone is trying to break into our house, and my husband is going to shoot him if he tries again. Please help us!"

My mom gives the officer on the phone all the information they ask of her—who are all in the house, how long this has been going on, and our address—before begging them to hurry.

From the corner of my eye, I can see my cousin Harry standing in the kitchen pointing his rifle at the side door. At first glance, he seems awfully calm, but as I turn and stare a little more intently, I can see the sweat dripping down his forehead.

"Don't get out of that car!" I hear my dad saying to the air from the front door. "Don't let me see you again."

I can no longer hear anything over my own heart pounding in my chest.

"Please, God, deliver us from evil," I mutter another prayer. "Please don't let that man get out of his car."

Suddenly I hear sirens in the distance. They start off faint then quickly get louder as they near my home.

When the siren's volume finally overtakes my own heartbeat, I hear a car engine revving outside and tires screech as someone speeds away.

The world goes silent.

"You can put your guns down," Frank says. "He's gone."

I let out a heavy breath I haven't even realized I'm holding, and Harry drops down to his knees as his rifle clatters to the floor. Ruby quickly collects the guns from all of us and takes them back to the master bedroom, while Lisa runs to me and buries herself in my arms.

The screaming police sirens come to an abrupt halt in front of our house. I see two officers walking around the back of our house as I hear my father inviting the other policemen in.

"What happened, Mr. Turman?" one officer asks.

"A man in a taxi trespassed on my property and made himself a threat to my family, so I had prepared to take matters into my own hands."

"Your wife said you had been armed?"

"That is correct."

"Do you have licenses for your guns?" the officer asks.

Frank nods. "Yes, I do."

"May we see them please?"

As my father goes to retrieve his papers, the police officers begin to ask us questions. We told him all that we know. That he is tan-skinned, about six feet tall, with brown eyes and shaggy dark hair.

"Did you notice the cab number on the side of the car?" another officer asks.

"No, sir," Harry says.

"Would you recognize him if you saw him again?"

Harry nods. "Yes, sir."

After a few more minutes of questioning, Frank emerges with a folder and hands it to one of the officers.

"Well, everything seems to be in order," the officer says after looking over the papers. He hands the folder back to Frank, and he and his partner head for the door. As his partner exits, the other officer turns back to us one last time.

"You're a lucky man, Mr. Turman," he says. "But know this: you have a right to defend your family and your home, but you had better hope if you ever take the shot, that they fall inside your house. Otherwise, you will be the one facing murder charges."

My father stares at the officer silently, his expression emotionless. The officer is the first to turn away.

"Have a good day, Mr. Turman."

"He's still out there!" Frank says as the officer walks away.

"We'll find him." With a tip of his cap, the officer gets into his car and drives away.

Frank closes the door, sits down on the sofa, and goes back to watching TV. The rest of us stand there, staring at one another and off into the distance.

I feel Lisa shaking in my arms. I slowly rub her back as my mind races. What just happened? It has all happened so quickly, and it was just one move away from going horribly wrong.

After several minutes go by, there's another knock at the front door.

The group who have just finally begun to relax after the incident about ten minutes prior all tense up again.

Frank looks at all of us, hesitant, before getting up and then walking over to the front door. He looks out the window and furrows his eyebrows.

"Dad?" I say. "Who is it?"

Frank opens the door and on their porch stands the same officer from before.

"We spotted him, Mr. Turman," the officer says. "He was parked around the corner, waiting for us to leave."

"So is he in your custody?"

The officer is silent.

"You didn't arrest him?" Frank yelled. "I'm telling you, he was up to no good!"

The officer sighs. "I agree with you, Mr. Turman, he clearly had ill intentions, but we have nothing to prove that. Nothing to hold him on or even detain him. All he did was walk up to your house and sit in his car, and that's not against the law."

The expression on my father's face distorted into a look of pure fury, meanwhile the rest of us gains a shared sense of despair.

"Nevertheless," the officer says before Frank has a chance to speak. "I can assure you, no one in this room will ever have to worry about that cab driver again. When I was talking to him, I told him that he was just another bad decision away from being maggot food. That there were several men inside that house locked and loaded. And if he had tried to enter that house or even walked up to it one more time, he would have gotten riddled with bullets. He went white as a sheet. Started stuttering and apologizing for harassing you. He asked me to tell you that he was so sorry for his actions and he would never bother you again."

"Is that supposed to reassure me?" Frank says.

"We'll be watching him, Mr. Turman. We know who he is, and he knows we do. I suspect he is going to be on his best behavior for some time." He looks at the rest of us. "Have a good day, everyone." As the officer walks away once more, Frank closes the door and faces us.

"Let this be a lesson to all of you," he said. "In stressful times, never panic. Stay focused and clear-minded, always be prepared, have a plan of action, try to think two or three steps ahead of your adversary, and do not be afraid to act. This may save your life one day."

CHAPTER 4

The Tainted Menu

Jeffrey[2] walks down the hall of the Ambrosia Chocolate Factory.[3] The sweet smell of chocolate permeates throughout the building. Like a fine wine, the chocolate has a sophisticated scent and flavor with an aroma of vanilla, banana, and vinegar. It's a pleasant odor that even spreads throughout the entire neighborhood. His work shift from 11:00 p.m. to 7:30 a.m. as a laborer is about to begin. The steady paycheck of $8.25 an hour and the overnight shift give Jeffrey the stability and freedom he needs to continue his hobby. He needs money to lure and entice his victims and to purchase the triazolam drug he would put in their drinks.

The night shift also allows him to work during a time when fewer supervisors and fellow employees are around and he doesn't have to make contact with the public. He

---

² Myers, Brian. October 28, 2021. "The Serial Killer Who Once Worked in a Chocolate Factory." Grunge. https://www.grunge.com/646366/the-serial-killer-who-once-worked-in-a-chocolate-factory/.

³ "VK.com | VK." n.d. M.vk.com. Accessed September 19, 2023. https://vk.com/wall-85378351_26591?lang=en.

doesn't have any associates, which is good, since he lacks trust in other people. Friendless and alone, Jeffrey silently walks the halls of Ambrosia.

But he's not alone, not really.

He's holding a carrying case in his right hand. He passes several coworkers. They smile and nod at Jeffrey as he walks by. He continues to walk down the hall and up to his locker. He opens it and places the carrying case inside before unzipping it and slowly lifting out a human skull. He decides to bring this friend along with him to work today.

Jeffrey begins to talk to the skull, reliving the memories he's had from mere hours ago. Leaning in, Jeffrey presses his lips against the cold, lifeless skull, kissing it goodbye, before placing it back in the carrying case, zipping it up, and closing the locker door.

He then walks to his working station and starts mixing the chocolate, the residue of the skull still on his hands.[4]

After several hours, Jeffrey and his fellow coworkers make their way to the lunch room for their break time. Jeffrey sits down at a lunch table and proceeds to pull out a dish with a strange type of meat slathered in sauce. He starts to eat his meal, savoring each and every bite.

His coworkers watch as he devours the meat, all of them baffled by his choice of food and the pure joy he is displaying while consuming his prepared dish. Despite its unappealing visual, they figure it must be good to cause such a strong reaction in him.

---

4   Fresh Meat: Jeffrey Dahmer. n.d. Documentary. Tubi.

Eventually, some of his coworkers build up enough courage to ask Jeffrey about his food. [5]

Jeffrey says, "It's my special gravy that makes it taste so good."[6]

They stare at the meat that Jeffrey continues to plunge his fork into and then place into his mouth. They watch him savoring the taste, and one of them asks him if they can have a piece of his meat to sample.

"No," Jeffrey says without hesitation before going back to his meal.

When lunch was over, he walks back to his station and starts the work process all over again. Shortly after he begins to start working again, a fellow employee notices that Jeffrey has fallen asleep on the job. The supervisor is notified. Jeffrey is awakened and escorted back into the manager's office, where he is asked why he fell asleep on the job.

"I can never sleep when I need to," he says.

"Why not?"

"Because I work the night shift. I have to do most things during the daytime, which prevents me from getting any sleep when I am supposed to."

He can't tell his boss the whole truth on why he rarely sleep, so partial truth will have to do.

His supervisor eventually accepts Jeffrey's excuses and sends him back to work. Jeffrey tries his best to stay awake,

---

[5] Davis, Don. 1995. *The Jeffrey Dahmer Story: An American Nightmare.* New York: St. Martin's Paperbacks.

[6] "The Story of the Beautiful Meal"| NextThought." n.d. Www.nextthought. com. Accessed September 19, 2023. https://www.nextthought.com/thoughts/ 2016/04/parable-9-the-story-of-the-beautiful-meal.

but his schedule just won't allow for a significant time of rest. Eventually it costs him this job that he works at for four years. This comes as a blow to Jeffrey, but at the end of the day, there is nothing he can do. He makes a choice: it is either his hobby or sleep, and it is his insatiable lust for blood and the companionship of the dead that prevails.

CHAPTER 5

A Lovers Quarrel

Some time has passed since the attempted home invasion. Lisa and I are cuddling together on a love seat in the den and watching a videotape of the blockbuster movie *Top Gun*. Lisa starts to fidget with her fingernails. I can sense a problem is brewing. She looks intently at me with great concern and then turns away. While deep in thought, she hangs her head down and starts to whisper to herself. I can't understand what she's saying. I can tell that something is wrong and something's bothering her. After a few minutes, I build up enough courage to ask the palpable question.

"What's wrong?"

That question gets Lisa's undivided attention. She stops fidgeting, lifts her head, and looks at me.

"You know, this is the first time that I have been here since that guy tried to break in. I feel so uncomfortable right now."

I knew it. I knew something was wrong. I have a sinking feeling in my gut that this isn't going to turn out well. This is not going to be quick and easy. This is going to be a long and impassioned conversation. I guess I should just turn off the television because that's the end of us watching the movie *Top Gun*. Man, I sure hate to stop watching it. I am really into that movie. Oh well, it's the right thing to do. Besides, I won't be able to enjoy it anyway. She needs reassurance that everything is going to be okay. So I turn off the VCR, walk over to the television, and turn that off too. Sitting back down, I take a deep breath, and with great solicitude, I grab Lisa's hand to comfort her.

"Don't be afraid. You have nothing to worry about. I will protect you. You can just call me Allstate because you're in good hands."

I smile at her and stare into her brown eyes looking for reassurance that my words of humor and comfort have worked. She still looks lost and miserable, but she nods her head anyways.

"Okay," she says.

I feel a sudden sense of great relief.

That wasn't bad at all. Good job, Jerome! I say to myself. *You handled that pretty well.*

Thinking the conversation is over, I walk back over to the television, turn it on, and walk back to the love seat. After sitting down next to Lisa, I reach for the VCR remote, lean back, and push the on button. The videocassette recorder powers back on, and after a few seconds I press play, and the flickering images of the blockbuster movie permeate throughout the room. My mind quickly drifts back to the plot of the movie, and I once again start to get lost in the show. However, my joyful movie experience is short-lived. After a few minutes, she turns and looks at me.

"You crave attention."

"What?"

I am shocked by Lisa's latest statement. I don't see that coming. Why is she saying that? I have a feeling that this is going to be really bad.

"You love it when women fawn all over you."

I look stunned by her accusation and respond with the first thing that pops into my head.

"Excuse me?"

I know that is not a well-thought-out response, but what else can I say? I am totally baffled by this latest round of questioning. But if I think that is bad, just wait until you hear what's coming next. Nothing kills the mood quicker than her next statement. I know it's coming.

"You don't love me anymore."

There it is! Oh well, movie night is over! I don't know what I've done to deserve this line of questioning, but I am sure that I am about to find out. So once again I reach for the remote and turn off the VCR. I then walk over to the television and turn it off as well. I walk back over to Lisa to sit down and focus on her present concerns. I look at Lisa, grab her hand, squeeze it gently, and hope to end this discussion as quickly as possible before it blows up. I foolishly try to say something cliché, which every man says when confronted with this volatile situation.

"Of course I still love you, honey."

That's a good response, I think to myself.

Now if I can just stop right there, everything may work out fine. Maybe this night may have a happy ending. But no! I go too far. I have to open my big mouth and ask the dumbest question of all.

"Why would you say that?"

As soon as I say it, I know it is a huge mistake. I want to kick myself for letting that slip. I've just opened the door for Lisa to tell me everything I don't want to hear. I am about to get a full report on my stupidity, and it will probably be well-deserved. Now I don't even want to hear her response because I know I have probably done something wrong. I don't know what I've done yet, but I have to just brace myself for the impact. I am just going to have to take it. I must prepare myself for the countless number of apologies that I am going to have to bombard her with for the rest of the night.

Lisa looks at me and says, "Why would I say that? Look at you!"

In utter confusion, I look at myself and shrug my shoulders.

She continues, "You just want all the women to love you."

I turn my head, lower my eyes, and contemplate her statement.

"Why do you need that? Why can't I be enough for you?"

Is she right? I haven't really thought about that before. I have to admit that I do like the attention, but I can't let her know that. So what should I say? I am at a loss for words. I better think of something quick. If I pause too long, she will know that she's right. Okay, I know what to do. I'll play dumb.

"What are you talking about?"

Lisa stands up with a face contorted with rage and put her hands on her hips. I suddenly realize that is not the right answer. I have just pushed the wrong button. She is able to see right through that response.

"I'm sick of this! I can't put up with this anymore!

She starts to pace around the room. I have to do something. I have to fix this. So I stand up and rub my forehead. I'm trying to think of a quick response, something that will calm her down. But the more I think about it, the more I start to get defensive and eventually say the wrong thing.

"Where is this coming from?"

Lisa stops pacing, looks at me, and says, "You almost got us killed the last time you performed."

"What did I do?" I look confused and distraught.

Lisa starts pacing again. She stops in front of me and says, "You know what I'm talking about! This obsession of yours to always be in the spotlight. Well, you got more than you expected the last time you performed, didn't you!"

I am starting to get annoyed and even more defensive.

"Are you trying to blame me for what happened here?"

"Stop it, Jerome! You know it's true. It's your fault because you have to be the center of attention. It's all about you! You want to be on stage, you need to be on stage because you love that all those women are screaming your name."

I realize that this is starting to get out of hand. She's really upset. I need to start saying the right things. Maybe if I try to make contact with her. I could touch her shoulder or stroke her hair. But I convince myself that first I must deny everything.

"That's not true!"

I try to reach for her hand, but she pulls it away.

"Don't lie to me! I hate this! Why can't it be just the two of us? Why can't you be happy with just me? Why do you need those women to want you?"

Lisa starts to cry. I put my arms around her shoulder to try and comfort her. She doesn't pull away. I feel terrible that I have caused her to cry. I start beating myself up inside and begin to question everything I am saying and doing.

I am an idiot. I keep saying the wrong things, I think to myself. *That last response was a disaster too. I am striking out. I can't seem to say or do anything right. I am just going to try and speak from the heart.*

"Don't say that. I love you. I don't want anyone else."

Lisa looks at me with pure disappointment and says, "If that was true, you wouldn't be shaking your butt in front of hundreds of people."

Wow, I had that coming.

"It's a job! That's all."

She pulls away from me, wipes her eyes, lifts her head, clears her throat, and gains her composure.

"Well, that job almost got us killed! Your need for attention got the interest of the wrong person, and you put me in the middle of it. You dragged me into your crazy world."

Wow! She is really making a great case. I usually don't lose arguments, but she is shooting down every excuse I come up with. I am clearly losing this discussion, but I can't let her know that or she will win this argument and force me to choose between my career or doing the right thing. So I continue to fight. I will plead my case. I will refuse to accept responsibility.

"That wasn't my fault! I can't help it that some nutjob tried to break into our house."

She can't blame me for someone else's perverted actions, so I feel good about that response. I start to smile inside. I'm thinking that if I can just get her to see my side of the story, maybe we can find some kind of compromise, but she refuses to budge from her position.

"It wouldn't have happened if you weren't performing in the first place."

She's right again. I just can't win this argument. But I keep trying.

"I can't believe you are saying this. What am I supposed to do?"

Another stupid question on my part. You would think that I would eventually learn my lesson.

"You are supposed to keep me safe! Did you do that the last time we were here, or did you put me in the line of fire?"

That is not the question I am expecting from her. What a relief. However, that question hurts. That is a low blow.

"That's not fair. I didn't ask for this."

Lisa walks up to me and says, "But it happened anyway. I can't live like this. Always looking over my shoulder. Living in fear." She looks deep into my eyes. "Jerome, you have to make a decision. It's either me or the stage. You can't have both."

There it is! That's the question that I was expecting. I knew it was coming to this. I've dreaded this moment. I am torn up inside. I can feel the apprehension taking control of my mind. The stress is building throughout my whole body. I am in total disarray. I am now wondering if she can tell that she just floored me with those words. Have I just become completely transparent? Can she see right through me? Am I now wearing my heart on my sleeve? It doesn't take long for me to get an answer to my question. I see her facial expression change because of the stunned look that has now come over my face. She can tell that I am shocked by her ultimatum. She can now read me like a book because I am emotionally distraught both inside and out. I am feeling weak and nauseous. My head starts spinning. My world is turning upside down. I've known it's been coming, but I still can't believe what Lisa has just said to me. I haven't seen this entire conversation coming at all today. I haven't even known that the incident bothered her. She has never said anything about it after that day. What am I going to do? I don't want to lose her, she's the first girl that I've ever loved, but I am not giving up show business. What can I do? What can I say? How can I solve this problem? I try to buy some time, so I start to pace back and forth rubbing my forehead.

I am trying to think of a solution. She's still standing in the same spot waiting for my answer. This is going to be the biggest decision I have ever made. Then it hits me. I have finally come to a conclusion. I know what I am going to do. So I stop pacing, walk up to her, reach for her hand, look into her eyes, and lie right to her face.

"I choose you!"

Lisa smiles and wraps her arms around me and holds me tight.

I whisper into her ear, "I'm done. I don't need this life. I will never perform again."

CHAPTER 6

Blood Bath

It's a cold, blustery summer night in Southeast Wisconsin. The moon is full and bright, illuminating the city. Depraved and revolting monstrous people are lurking in the shadows and preparing for the kill. An unwitting victim sits in a reclining, sofa-like chair and waits for Jeffrey to bring him his venomous drink and fifty dollars that he's promised him in trade for posing for some diagrammatic pictures.

While he waits apprehensively, Jeffrey is in the kitchen standing in front of the counter and crushing some triazolam, a light hypnotic sedative, with a can of beer that he has promised his prey. He looks back to see if the unsuspecting pawn is watching him. After crushing the tablets, he grabs a clear tall glass from the kitchen cupboard's middle shelf. He pops open the beer can, and the excess carbonated pressure rushes out with a hissing sound as a cool wet spray echoes and infuses throughout the room. The alcohol starts to fill the glass as the bubbly foam rises to the top and then settles down before spilling over. The glass fills up, and the strong aromatic scent of the hops and barley, which resembles an earthy overripe fruit, starts to spread throughout the kitchen. Jeffrey then attentively sweeps the pulverized powderlike triazolam conscientiously into the glass of beer, making sure not to leave any residue behind. He takes another glance at the sofa and wipes down the kitchen counter with a cloth thoroughly.

Jeffrey uses his index finger to mix the triazolam into the beer, making sure it's entirely dissolved. Once the substance is fully integrated in the liquid, he takes out his finger, wipes off the mixture, and stares into the invisible poisoned glass. He visualizes with great anticipation for the night that awaits his oblivious recipient. Jeffrey then pours a glass of beer for himself and starts to carry both glasses into the living room. He is careful not to mix up the two drinks and attentively remembers that the right hand is carrying the tainted drink so he doesn't poison himself. When he walks in, he smiles at the young man and hands him his glass. Jeffrey watches as he drinks the entire cup in one gulp. After a brief period of time, the young man starts to slur his words, he becomes drowsy, his coordination is off making it hard to move, the room starts to spin, and his vision is hazy. He tries to gather his composure, to no avail, and eventually he slouches back on the sofa as he succumbs to the drug, leaving Dhamer in full control of his whole body.

Jeffrey slowly creeps toward him and hovers over his prey, reaches out his strong hands, and places them around the victim's throat. Pressing down, he starts to squeeze, applying more pressure with each passing second. The young man tries to desperately squirm free from his captor like a fish on a hook. Jeffrey, while squeezing on the throat of this struggling man, forces him out of the chair and takes him to the floor. Jeffrey then pins the victim's arms to the ground with his knees and continues to apply pressure to his neck. The scared young man eventually surrenders and succumbs to the violence perpetrated against him and passes out.

Jeffrey continues to apply great pressure to the man's throat until his vital organs begin to shut down. His air passages have been cut off for so long that his tongue begins to swell and his lips turn dark blue. After several more minutes pass, Jeffrey starts to loosen his grip. He looks down at the limp, lifeless body staring back at him. He begins to feel a sense of satisfaction as he realizes that he has just strangled this young man to death. This young man has fought until his will to live ran out and the shadows of death overtook him. And now, Jeffrey can have his fun.

After satisfying his carnal desires with the lifeless corpse, he realizes that he has to hide the evidence. Jeffrey hears his grandmother's peaceful snores from her bedroom as he carries the dead boy into the bathtub and starts to dissect the body.

He grabs a hacksaw and starts to chip away at the limbs, removing them one by one. The blood flows from the dead body and runs down the drain, self-cleaning the mess that he has created.

After detaching the extremities, he starts to sever the head from the body. He takes great pleasure in removing this body part, and once he rips the head off the torso, he lifts it up and places it in front of his face. He stares into the eyes and admires his work. He places it aside and finishes hacking the rest of the body into smaller pieces. After, he carries the remains into the basement's fruit cellar and stores them there for a few days until he has time to finish the job.

He walks back upstairs and goes to bed. With a clear conscience, he sleeps like a baby.

After several days, Jeffrey's grandmother starts to smell death trickle throughout the house. She's so disgusted by the stomach-sickening stench that she harshly questions Jeffrey about the horrific odor. He promises to promptly fix the problem. Realizing that he is running out of time to remove the remains of his latest victim, he purchases a can of acid in order to dissolve the flesh from off the bones. He walks down into the fruit cellar, puts the body into a vat that is standing upright, and pours the acid into the large container over the body parts, and watches the dead flesh start to sizzle and fade away, leaving only the skeletal remains. He then begins to smash the bones with a hammer until they are ground up into dust. However, he saves the skull intact as a memento.

He sweeps up the skeletal dust into plastic bags and carries them to the dump. He places the skull in a metal box for safekeeping, taking great care to hide it in a place his grandmother would never look.

CHAPTER 7

Heart Break

It's a warm, cloudy summer night. I am performing at the famous Milwaukee Summer Festival. I can smell the stench of cigarette smoke in the air. The delicious aroma of beer and brats permeates the festival grounds.

It's approaching midnight. I am standing backstage. Stagehands and other performers are frantically rushing past me. I am just behind the main curtain. I can hear the fans screaming. My heart is pumping with excitement as I wait for my introduction. Then it hits me. A sudden surge of guilt overwhelms me. My thoughts shift from the present moment, which's been filled with excitement and exhilaration, to an earlier conversation I had with Lisa that is now causing me great pain and guilt over the horrendous lie that I have previously told my first true love.

Was Lisa right? I stare off into the abyss contemplating this soul-searching question. *Am I obsessed with the adulation of my fans, especially the women?*

I look around at the women that are backstage. I see several watching me. They are smiling. My heart races with excitement. I blush. They wave at me. I wave back.

What's wrong with me? I drop my head into my hands in frustration. *Why can't I stop? Look at me.* I look down at my black outfit and sequin glove and shake my head in disgust. *Here I am again*, while looking around at my surroundings. "I am risking everything just to perform." I start to contemplate the consequences of my actions and reflect on the depths I have fallen just to do this. *I am lying to Lisa and performing behind her back. I am coming up with excuses every time I sneak out.* I think about our conversation earlier that day, when I held her hand and looked into her eyes and told her that I was visiting with family and checking on my sick grandfather tonight. *I am going to get caught eventually. This can only last so long. Why am I doing this? This isn't my future, she is.*

My mind drifts into a beautiful future. I see Lisa and I standing in front of a big white house. We are holding hands. I see four children running and playing together in the large front yard. The two boys are spitting images of me when I was a child. The two girls look as beautiful as their mother. I'm happy. Lisa and I are smiling because we have the perfect life. But then I wake up from the fantasy and look around at my reality.

This is it! This is my last one! I am done after tonight!

My thoughts come to an end when the MC takes the stage. It's time to focus on the here and now. I have a show to perform. I can't let my fans down. If I make one wrong step, one awkward turn, or one misguided spin, the whole routine is ruined. My reputation is at risk, not to mention the insults after the show from everyone watching. I hear the MC tapping the microphone. He clears his voice.

"Ladies and gentlemen, this is what you all have been waiting for, our main event. Please give a round of applause for Milwaukee's Michael Jackson, Mr. Jerome Turman!"

The house lights go dark. A few seconds pass before the stage lights shine bright illuminating my presence on the stage. The fans go wild, screaming as loud as they can. I can't believe that people would get that excited over someone just pretending to be a national celebrity. But that's how popular Michael Jackson was in the eighties. If you resemble him and can dance like him, you can actually jump-start your career in show business. I know it is only temporary, but it is a start. I look at it as a stepping stone to bigger and better things in the future. The music starts, and I perform another show. The crowd goes wild. The women are throwing their clothes onto the stage. The men are singing along. The children are dancing in the aisles. It's a beautiful sight to see.

The show comes to a dramatic conclusion with explosions and flashing lights. I am breathing hard and sweating profusely. The show is over. The night has come to an end. The extreme satisfaction of a successful show is exhilarating. After the performance, I walk off the stage to greet my adoring fans. One by one dozens of people walk up to me, extending their hands. I reach out and clasp hands with each and every one of them. We exchange pleasantries and talk as if we are old friends. We laugh and smile together. It's such a wonderful moment in my life. Everyone is so nice and warm. Many of them want autographs. I gladly sign their posters and sheets of paper. The women want to kiss me on the cheek and they want me to sign their arms and legs. They want to take pictures with me. I never turn them down. I am always a willing participant. Two women approach me. One of them extends her open palms toward me.

"May I have a hug?"

"Of course you can."

She stretches out her arms, wraps them around my shoulders, and draws me close to her heart. I can feel her heart pounding with excitement. I can smell her perfume. It has a sweet-smelling aroma. Suddenly I feel a powerful blow to the side of my head. Immediately pain shoots through my nervous system. It's emanating from my face and permeating through my entire body. I can even feel it in my toes. The impact causes me to stagger backward. My jaw goes numb. I see tiny stars before my eyes. I quickly realized that someone has hit me. Someone has just punched me in the face, really hard. The crowd around me gasps in horror. The girl who was hugging me has let go and has placed her hands over her mouth. She is just as shocked as I am. I try to shake it off. It takes a few seconds for me to regain my balance and the conscious awareness of my current surroundings. After I am able to clear my eyes and refocus my vision, I see several people, who are standing around me, pointing to someone walking away. I look at the person they have identified as my assailant. To my surprise, he is not running away but just slowly walking through the crowd. I can't believe it. Someone has just punched me in the face and is just casually walking away. I am furious. I start to run toward him. The crowd is chasing behind me. I grab him from behind, raise my fist to strike a blow, and prepare to throwdown. Suddenly I see the face of my attacker. I am shocked by what I see. The person standing in front of me is not a stranger. It's not even a man. It's my girlfriend, Lisa. My legs and arms go limp, my mind goes numb, and my heart is completely broken. The crowd catches up to me and quickly stands between the two of us. I look at Lisa with pain and anger in my tearful eyes.

"Why! Why would you do this!"

Lisa looks at me. She's furious. I can see the anger in her eyes. But I can also see the tears flowing down her face as well.

"You lied to me!"

I am still in great pain and stunned by the revelation that Lisa was the assailant. I am so angry, but I know she is right. This is all my fault. Should I apologize and beg for her forgiveness? That would be the smart thing to do, but what about all these people watching? What would they think? I can't let them think that this violent action is acceptable. I have to say something.

"That gives you no right to hit me! Especially in front of hundreds of people!"

Lisa looks around at the crowd and says, "Is this what you want? Well, you can have it."

With tears in her eyes, she turns around, leaves the area, slowly vanishing into the darkness, and completely walks out of my life. I never see Lisa again.

CHAPTER 8

The Night Stalker

Jeffrey dresses to hit the town. He's standing in the bedroom of his grandmother's house and buttoning his shirt. At his feet lie the remnants of a previously dismembered body. Skeletal souvenirs from his previous encounters with unwitting victims. He nonchalantly steps over them, walks over to his canvas shoes, and easily slips them on, then walks back over to his prize possessions, picks them up, admires them, places them back in the file cabinet, and locks them up to keep them hidden. He enthusiastically works his way to the front door and waves goodbye to his loving grandmother. She smiles graciously and waves back, watching proudly as her grandson walks out the front door and closes it behind him.

Jeffrey walks the streets of downtown Milwaukee, the moon high in the night sky. He loves frequenting the many bars on the city's east side. On this night, he sets his sights on one that's dimly lit like a candle flickering in the night. The bars' subdued characteristic is camouflaged by the loud music disseminating throughout the neighborhood.

It's drawing Jeffrey into its allure. He doesn't resist and enters the club.

Jeffrey scans the environment with his piercing blue eyes and takes a lap around the crowded nightclub before he settles into a secluded corner. He watches the people as they come and go, looking for someone who appeals to him, someone vulnerable and with whom he can connect emotionally, or at least pretend to. It's what most people do, play pretend. No one ever shows their true self. It's just the way the world works.

Jeffrey pours on the charm with persuasiveness in an attempt to coax his prey and lure them into a false sense of security. He needs to get them to lower their guard so he can seduce them with an enticing proposition, like a spider perched high in its web waiting for its next meal.

One man approaches him. "Hi," he says.

"Hello," Jeffrey responds.

"I hope you are having a good time tonight. Let us know if you want anything to drink." Jeffrey recognizes him as the maître d'. "I'll have a beer." The maître d' looks toward the bar and signals to the bartender. The bartender is using a towel to clean his work area. When he looks up and sees the maître d' signaling to him, he nods his head in approval.

He finishes wiping off a glass, places it on the counter, and then uses the towel to wipe his hands. After setting the towel down next to the glass, he walks away from the bar and approaches Jeffrey and the maître d'. "How can I help you?"

"Take this gentleman's order please," the maître d' said.

"Yes, sir." The bartender looks at Jeffrey and says, "What would you like?"

"I'll have a beer."

"Coming right up."

The bartender turns away from Jeffrey, walks over to the bar, and grabs a cold can of beer and a large frosted mug. He then walks over to Jeffrey, reaches into the pocket of his apron, pulls out a coaster, and places it on the small round table next to Jeffrey's chair, setting the chilled beer mug on top. He then cracks open the can of beer, and a hissing spray of moisture perfumes the air with alcohol, and the smell of a fruity, fresh aroma of hops. The bartender then starts to carefully pour the golden, light, bubbly liquid into the mug. The glass slowly fills up with beer and glistens under the house lights as it foams at the top.

Jeffrey looks at the mug and wets his lips. He reaches into his pocket, pulls out some cash, and pays the bartender. Taking it, the bartender walks away.

Jeffrey leans back and starts to drink his beer. He scans the club for his next victim. The more he drinks, the bolder he becomes. Soon, he has lost all his inhibitions. It's time to act.

He leaves his secluded corner and starts to patrol the nightclub like a shark circles its victims. He spots a suitable choice and moves in for the kill.

"Hello," Jeffrey says. "My name is Jeff."

The man turns to him. "Hello."

They engage in a few minutes of friendly conversations before Jeffrey sees his opportunity.

"Have you ever thought about modeling?" Jeffrey says, "You know I'm a photographer. We should head over to my place and get some beers. I would love to take some pictures of you."

The man hesitates to respond.

"I will pay you fifty bucks for the photos," Jeffrey quickly responds.

Despite the hesitation in his eyes, the man agrees to take the money. Jeffrey has succeeded in luring this man away from the herd. The two leave the bar and proceed to head toward Jeffrey's house of horrors.[7]

---

[7] "Confessions of a Serial Killer." 2014. MSNBC.com. https://www.msnbc.com/documentaries/watch/confessions-of-a-serial-killer-332865091922.

CHAPTER 9

Looking For Love In All
The Wrong Places

Immediately after the incident at Summerfest, I get in my parents' car and start to drive back home (no more cab rides for me). I am completely lost in my thoughts.

I can't believe she did that! She hit me! I start scratching my head and tapping my thumb on the steering wheel. *I can't believe she hit me in front of all those people. That was so embarrassing. They'll never ask me to come back. I will never be able to perform there again. I hope the media wasn't there. What if someone took a picture? If this gets out, I can never show my face again. She ruined everything!*

Suddenly, I realize something very alarming. *How did she know that I was performing at Summerfest tonight? Who told her?* Then it hit me. *Harry! It must have been him. It had to be him. Who else could it be? That dirty rat.*

I can feel the anger building inside. *Wait until I get home. I'm going to confront him and ask him why he would do that to me.* I start to accelerate and drive recklessly trying to quickly get home.

When I arrive, I pull up to the house and into the driveway. I turn off the car, open the driver-side door, and run to the house. I place the house key into the lock with urgency before bursting into my home. I am on a mission to find my cousin and confront him. I call out his name.

"Harry!" He doesn't answer. I call out his name again. "Harry!" Still, he doesn't respond. "Where are you?"

I look into his bedroom. It's empty. He's not there, but I see his wallet on his nightstand. He must be home. He doesn't go anywhere without his wallet. So I check the bathroom and the kitchen. Still no sign of him. I look out of the kitchen window to see if he's in the backyard. I only see two squirrels running back and forth. The last place to look is downstairs in the basement, which has been turned into a rec room. I quickly walk down the basement stairs, and I turn to my left, and lo and behold, I see him standing behind his keyboard with his headphones on. He sees me and smiles.

"Hey, Jerry, you gotta hear this new song I just finished writing. It's awesome."

I walk over to him angrily. "Why did you tell Lisa that I was performing at the Summerfest grounds tonight? How could you do that to me? You knew that I didn't want her to know. I told you that I didn't want her to know that I was still performing. I trusted you."

Harry looks confused. "What are you talking about?"

I menacingly look at him. "She was there!"

Harry is shocked. "No way! What happened?"

"She hit me!"

Harry drops the headphones on the table. "She did! Where?"

"In the face."

Harry stares at the side of my face and sees the bruise. "Man, that looks bad. You should put some ice on that."

I quickly tire of this banter. I want to get back to the real issue. The reason I raced home in the first place.

"Why did you tell her that I was performing at Summerfest?"

Harry looks at me with a straight face and says, "Jerry, I didn't tell her anything. I don't talk to her."

I look dazed and confused. I was sure he did it. "Well, how did she find out about it?"

Harry starts to reflect and says. "Well, Aunt Ruby was talking to her over the phone the other day. Ask your mom. She might have told her. Did she know where you were performing tonight?"

I drop my head and look extremely dejected. "Yeah, she knew."

Harry puts his hand on my shoulder. "Let's put some ice on that before the swelling gets worse."

We walk up the stairs. I sit down on the kitchen chair. Harry opens the freezer door, grabs several ice cubes, and places them into a sandwich bag. He walks over to me and hands me the bag.

"Here, put this on your face and hold it there until the slight swelling goes down."

I take the bag and place it on the side of my face. The ice is so cold. I don't know how long I am going to be able to stand the stinging sensation. I lift up my head and look at Harry.

"Man, I'm sorry. Please forgive me for accusing you of telling Lisa where I was."

Harry pats me on the back and says, "We're family. I would never betray you."

"Thanks, man."

Harry walks back over to the refrigerator, opens the door, and grabs a package of lunch meat. He walks over to the kitchen counter and makes a sandwich. Then with a mouthful of food, he says to me, "So now what? Are you going to confront Aunt Ruby?"

I quickly respond, "No way! She would kill me if I even considered confronting her about anything. Besides, even if I was able to build up enough courage to ask her about her conversation with Lisa, it would totally backfire against me."

Harry looks confused. "Why is that?"

"Because she would just give me this long, insulting, and humiliating speech about lying. I would just regret bringing up the subject in the first place."

We both laugh.

"So is it over between you and Lisa?"

I hesitate for a moment, thinking about all that had transpired that night. "Yeah, it's over."

I start to feel a great sense of loss. I try to fight back tears. I lower my eyes and drop my head. This is a pain that I have never felt before. It's gut-wrenching. I feel like someone just punched me in the stomach. There is a gaping hole where my heart used to be. I have all these emotions suddenly surging throughout my core. For the first time, I realize how much Lisa means to me, and now she's gone. I truly love her.

Harry looks at me and says, "I'm sorry, man."

I must try to gain my composure. I can't let Harry know that this is so painful. I take the ice bag off my face, place it on the kitchen table, and say, "Hey, I'm free! I can do and go anywhere I want to now." I start to smile. "You know what? I can also see whoever I want. I can start dating again."

Harry takes another bite. "So what do you want to do?"

"Well, first I want to start taking some jobs at places where there are a lot of women because I am free to mingle."

Harry finishes chewing his food and swallows. "You should just stick with the plan. It's been working for you so far."

I start to rub my hands together. "I want to take advantage of this opportunity. I want to meet some women."

"Jerome, you are obsessed with women."

I pause for a moment, drop my head, and start reflecting on my past. After a few seconds, I lift my head and say, "I know! It's my weakness. Besides, I want to have some fun."

After several minutes of thinking about where to perform next, I am hit with a revelation.

"I know where I need to go."

Harry takes another bite of his sandwich and says, "Where is that?"

I smile and say, "Northridge Mall!"

Harry abruptly gulps his food down his throat and drops his sandwich on the kitchen counter.

"Are you crazy! That's where people go to die!"

A detestable look of contestation settles over my face. "It's not that bad. Besides, you know that's where all the women go to shop and hang out."

Harry's expression and voice changes to deep concern and utter contempt for what I am proposing. "Man, it's bad over there! You know it's not safe. We haven't been there in years. Besides, Aunt Ruby won't let you take her car to Northridge. Especially after all the break-ins and car thefts. So how are you going to get there?"

I scratch my head. "I don't know. I hadn't thought about that. Maybe I'll just tell her that I'm performing at a mall. I don't have to tell her which mall. There are a lot of malls in Milwaukee. She doesn't need to know which one."

Harry shakes his head in frustration. "What if something happens?"

I quickly respond, "What could happen?"

"What if her car gets stolen while you are inside flirting with every female at the show?"

I roll my eyes. "The car will be fine. You worry too much. Besides, you'll be there. You can keep checking on it throughout the night."

Harry shakes his head in disagreement. "No way! I'm not going. You couldn't pay me enough to go back to that mall."

I look shocked. "What?! You're not going? Why not?"

Harry frowns and says, "I just told you."

I am in shock. I know he doesn't like the Northridge Mall, but I still can't believe he will allow that to keep him from going with me to the show.

"Come on, man! You've got to go. It's going to be so much fun. The nightclub over there has a dance floor and a bar. It's party time!"

Harry stands his ground. "I'm not going. I told you that it's not safe over there anymore."

I look disappointed. "Suit yourself. I'm calling my agent tomorrow, and I'm going to ask him to set up a gig for me at the Northridge Mall ASAP." I walk away and start singing to myself, "I'm going to the 'Ridge! I'm going to the 'Ridge! I'm going to the 'Ridge!"

CHAPTER 10

Ghost Mall

The haunting image of the Northridge Mall today is shocking. The abandoned ruins of the once-thriving shopping center is now looked upon as a ghost mall.[8] From the outside, it looks like the perfect location to shoot an episode of *The Walking Dead*. Trash is littered throughout the massive, vacant parking lot. Graffiti lines the walls of the massive structure. From the inside, it looks dead, like a scene right out of a zombie movie. There's vandalism throughout with broken glass on the now-motionless escalators and shattered windows on the food court atrium. Ankle-deep water rests along the floor, and mold accumulates where moviegoers use to watch blockbuster films at the mall's theater. It's cold and quiet inside. The only sign of life are the large decorative trees still growing in the center of the mall. The structure of the mall is still well-preserved, just waiting for someone to breathe life back into its lifeless

---

[8] "Inside a Ghost Mall: Northridge Sits Quietly, Unknown Future Ahead." 2012. OnMilwaukee. January 9, 2012. https://onmilwaukee.com/articles/northridgetour.

husk.[9] With just a push of a button, it might live again. Its history is one of initial success that gradually deteriorated and died because of crime, debilitating rumors, violence, and murder.

The eight-hundred-thousand-square-foot shopping center opened its doors in August of 1972. Northridge is located on the corner of Seventy-Sixth and Brown Deer Road. It sits just a few minutes from one of Milwaukee's most affluent suburbs, River Hills. Hundreds of thousands of people flocked to the gigantic mall over the first decade, including myself. It was built in a wealthy suburb of Milwaukee's northside. A beautiful area with lakes and restaurants. It was the place to go for shopping, socializing, eating, movies, and games. But in the mid- to late eighties, things started to slowly change. Rumors began to circulate throughout the city. I remember the stories about the numerous carjackings, robberies, assaults, and gang-related fights. Even the rumors of Lawrencia Bembenek hiding out in the Northridge parking lot, immediately after her escape from prison for allegedly killing a fellow officer's wife, were circulating the airwaves. The *Run, Bambi, Run* story was the most famous prison escape in Wisconsin history and one of the most nationally televised stories from Milwaukee.

However, the most terrifying rumor for me growing up was the one about the serial knife attacks at the Northridge Mall. Someone would hide underneath a parked car at night waiting for the owner to arrive. When the unsuspecting victim would try to unlock his car door,

---

9   "What Happened to Northridge Mall, and Why Is It Still There? Milwaukee Magazine." 2020. Www.milwaukeemag.com. February 11, 2020. https://www. milwaukeemag.com/happened-northridge-mall-still/.

the assailant would reach out from underneath the car and slice the victim's Achilles tendon with a butcher knife. The victim would cry out in agony and collapse to the ground. That would give the perpetrator the time to climb out from underneath the car and ambush the wounded victim. The assailant would attack, beat, and brutally stab the victim, take his money, and steal his car. That story terrified me as a young man. I believed it was not safe to shop, socialize, or even visit the Northridge area anymore.

Then on April 21, 1992, Jesse and Barbara Anderson left their home in Cedarburg, Wisconsin, around 6:30 p.m. and drove south toward the Northridge Mall. After a thirty-minute drive, they arrive in time to catch a seven-o'clock movie at the six-screen movie theater inside the mall. After the film, they headed over to the TGI Friday's restaurant that was located on the outer edge of the Northridge Mall parking lot. After dinner, while walking back to their car, Jesse suddenly pulls out a fishing knife and attacks his wife, stabbing her in the face and torso repeatedly. People started to flow toward the back of the restaurant when they heard a scream, but when they reached the crime scene, they stopped to find Barbara sprawled under a car, lying in a pool of blood with over twenty stab wounds throughout her upper body. They also found Jesse sitting beside his car with three stab wounds to his chest and the knife plunged deep into the palm of his hand. When the authorities and paramedics arrived, he begged them to help his wife. He tried to blame the murder on a robbery gone bad, but the police were suspicious and suspected him of the crime. He was eventually arrested and charged. He was later tried and found guilty of first-degree murder and sentenced to life in prison. Northridge Mall was forever stained by the Barbara Anderson murder.[10] It could never recover from such a violent attack.

But the horrors did not end there. Decades later, long after the mall had been abandoned, on the night of July 22, 2019, a maintenance worker who was hired to clean and fix up the dead mall would encounter a terrible accident. This enthusiastic breadwinner was the father of six children. He was a true handyman who always found ways to support his family. When he was offered the job to restore the mall, he seized the opportunity and went straight to work. He hired family and friends to work with him. He was a hard worker and started to bring optimism and respectability back to the old, decrepit mall. He welded doors shut and installed security cameras to make the mall safe again. The inside of the mall was starting to come back to life with his extensive cleaning efforts. However, that all came to an end on the night of July 22. As the esteemed employee and three of his coworkers were leaving the site around 9:00 p.m., he noticed that the door to the electrical box was open. He walked over to the box and attempted to close it. When he touched the box, a surge of electricity shot through his body. His brother-in-law pulled him away from the box,

---

[10] Schultz, Benjamin, and Jerald Podair. 2020. "'They're Moving North': Milwaukee, the Media, and the Murder of Barbara Anderson." https://ia902902.us.archive.org/17/items/theyremovingnorth-paper-20200312/They%27re%20Moving%20North%20paper.pdf.

but it was too late. This compassionate and caring man slumped to the floor, curled up into a ball, and died.[11]

It was a tragedy that happened to someone who was trying to help restore the luster of a crumbling shopping center. Whose walls are filled with terrifying stories and life-changing events.

There's one more horror story I know of to add to the dark history of this mall: my own.

----

[11] Carson, Sophie. n.d. "Man Electrocuted at Northridge Mall Leaves behind Six Children; Family Looking for Answers in Death." Journal Sentinel. Accessed September 23, 2023. https://www.jsonline.com/story/news/ local/2019/07/29/northridge-mall-electrocution-death-victor-diazs-family-tells-story/1844944001/.

CHAPTER 11

In The Devil's Crosshairs

The sun beats down on the single-family home built in 1939, in the pleasant West Allis neighborhood. The two souls residing in the West Allis house are worlds apart, serial killer Jeffrey Dahmer and his sweet grandmother.

The red, white, and brick home has a painted white door bearing a floral wreath with a box for the mail that, when opened, the mail fell directly into the home. Like the mail, Dahmer's victims would enter this home and leave like junk mail, torn into pieces, tossed out like garbage, and never to be seen again.

On this fateful day, Jeffrey's grandmother is serenely humming "Amazing Grace" and fiddling around in her kitchen like any normal morning. She pours the ice-cold water into the coffee maker, measuring the ground-up coffee beans into the filter, and starts to brew the coffee before starting to make breakfast.

After she finishes cooking, she calls out to her grandson, "Jeff, breakfast is ready, come and get it!" She waits for a reply, but he doesn't answer. After a few minutes, she decides to prepare her plate and start to eat.

She finishes eating and washing the dishes, yet there is still no sign of Jeffrey. She sighs before she moves to the living room.

Grabbing her Bible and reading glasses that are sitting on top of the end table next to the recliner, she begins to read the scriptures as she waits for her grandson to finally make an appearance.

"Jeffrey," she calls out again later. "The grass is getting long, so you need to mow the lawn today." She hesitates a few seconds and says, "Well, if you are not going to cut the grass today, are you going to church with me tonight for Bible study? She waits for an answer but never receives one.

Jeffrey ignores her cries because he's in his own little world. He sits alone in his bedroom, lounging on a stack of bunched-up pillows and spellbound by the movie he is watching on television. He's putting himself in a trance trying to get psyched up and kindled for the hunt.[12] A ritual he would repeat continuously over and over again before his killing escapades. On this day he's watching the horror movie called *The Exorcist*, once considered one of the scariest movies of all time.

His eyes are fixated on the flickering lights pulsating from the television screen as the electron beams emit all over the darkened room. Dahmer gets lost in the heat of the moment, his heart pounding with excitement from the terrifying images portrayed on the television screen.

---

[12] Shenfeld, Hilary. n.d. "How Serial Killers Get in the Mood for Murder." A&E. https://www.aetv.com/real-crime/serial-killer-rituals-prepare-to-murder-jeffrey-dahmer-btk-ted-bundy.

As Jeffrey meditates on the movie, it sends him into a hypnotic state and launches him into a brief paralyzing trance, causing him to start humming in a monotone manner. He then begins to slowly rock back and forth, with a steady rhythmic speed as time elapses. His blue eyes are soft and glazed over as if his state of mind has been captured by the movie's demonic monster.

His two favorite movies to watch were *The Exorcist* and *Return of the Jedi.* After hours of watching these movies over and over again, Jeffrey starts to gravitate toward the corrupt and degenerate characters from them. The creepy Emperor from 1983's *Return of the Jedi* and the eerie, satanic character in *The Exorcist* films become his idolic heroes. Jeffrey feels so connected to these characters because he's able to relate to their power of control over their mortal prey. He has become mesmerized by their evil and corrupt ways and obsesses over them as though they have special superpowers of dominance and suppression. His obsession metastasized throughout every fiber in his body as he began to morph into them. Both have yellow eyes, and Dahmer would sometimes wear yellow contact lenses to nightclubs when he went to hunt for potential victims. He wants to be more like them, and he ultimately wants to become them.[13]

After hours of psyching himself up for the kill, the connection is now complete with the Exorcist's antagonistic character, and he begins to feel as though he's one with the demonic villain. He's now ready for the hunt. He leans over to the bedside table, grabs the remote, and turns off

---

[13] "Why Were Jeffrey Dahmer's Eyes Yellow? Explaining His Signature Glasses and Yellow Contacts." 2022. Seventeen. October 3, 2022. https://www.seventeen.com/celebrity/movies-tv/a41502483/jeffrey-dahmer-glasses-monster/.

the television and gets out of bed. After getting dressed, he looks down and scans the room for his shoes. He sees them perched next to the dried-up human remains of the previous victims. He picks up the bones carefully, carries them over to a file cabinet, and places them gently inside before locking the cabinet and going back to put on his shoes.

He's ready for his evening plans, and this time, Jeffrey already has a person in mind. He looks down on the dresser and sees his personal drawing of an altar that he hopes to build. The drawing has the altar covered with skulls, lit by burning candles and featuring a blood-stained carving knife plunged deep into the dried-up skeletal remains of a previous victim. Beside the drawing, there is a flyer with pictures prominently displayed throughout the pamphlet. Inscribed on the flyer are the words "Come enjoy a night of pure excitement at the Northridge Mall as we present Milwaukee's own Michael Jackson impersonator Jerome Turman."

Jeffery picks up the flyer and stares with ravenous intent at the pictures before he places it in his pocket and heads out the door.

He's ready to meet his next victim: me.

CHAPTER 12

Setting The Stage

I'm in my bedroom laying out different clothing options for tonight's big show. Should I wear the red leather jacket, black pants, white socks, and black shoes? Or the black leather jacket, white shirt, red bow tie, black leather pants, white socks, and black shoes?

I furrow my eyebrows and purse my lips as I go back and forth. This show is a huge opportunity that can sky-rocket my career. Everything has to be perfect, down to the costume's very last detail. Eventually, I decide to try on those two and all my other outfits as well to see how they look and which one feels most authentic for tonight, while blasting "Billie Jean" and "Beat It" in the background on repeat. I find myself dancing to the music between costume changes, getting into character more and more after every listen-through. I let the music move me to my decision, and in the end, I go for the black jacket, white shirt, and red bow tie. As I look in the mirror one last time, I know I am making the right choice, the perfect outfit for what will soon be a perfect performance on a perfect night at Northridge Mall.

All I need now is someone to go with.

Harry won't make the show tonight, but there is no way I'm going to be hanging backstage after the show alone. So I head over to the phone on the nightstand by my bed. After a moment of consideration as to whom to hit up, I pick up the phone and dial.

"Hello?" I hear the voice of one of my best friends, Tim, on the other end, more chipper than usual.

"Hey, man!" I exclaim. "How's it going?"

The chipperness in Tim's voice deflates almost instantly. "Not much," he says. "Just chillin'."

My brow creases in suspicion. "You all right, bro? What's up?"

There's silence on the other end, before I finally hear a sigh of defeat. "I'm trying to hook up with this babe tonight, but she's not returning my calls."

I suddenly realize why he seems so disappointed it is me who called. The poor man's getting ghosted.

"How long have you been trying to hook up with this girl?" I ask.

More silence.

"Tim?"

"About a month," Tim confesses.

Ouch.

"Well, hey, I'm performing at Northridge tonight. You should come! There'll be plenty of shorties there for us to choose from!"

"I don't know..." Tim hesitates. "What if she calls back? I really like her."

"Man, let her go. You hook up with her now, and she'll hold all the power. You'll be chasing her forever."

I can tell he isn't fully on board yet. I sigh. No matter how bad I don't want to admit it, I understand. I'll be lying if I don't say I have looked over at the phone when it rang and wondered if it is Lisa. But I know I need to let go, and so does Tim.

"Let's go meet some new women, Tim. Women who want to be with us, who're not going to play games. Someone we don't have to chase."

I bite my lip, waiting for my friend's response.

"Okay, I'll go."

A wide smile creeps onto my face as I fist-bump the air.

"What time's the show?" Tim asks.

"I go on stage at nine o'clock, but the club opens at seven p.m.," I answer. "I'm getting to the club around eight forty-five, but I'll be heading over to the mall itself as soon as possible. There are going to be plenty of ladies shopping, and I want to be the first item on their holiday shopping list."

Through the phone, we both share a hearty laugh.

"All right, all right, I'll meet you at Northridge around six o'clock."

I fist-bump the air victoriously. "I'll meet you at the food court. See you later!"

Hanging up the phone, I sigh in relief. Part of the fun of performing is having someone to share the memories of that night. It just won't be the same if I'm riding solo. Plus, it's always nice to have a wingman.

The last decision I have to make is whether to wear a casual outfit to walk around the mall or actually wear my costume. It doesn't take long for me to make up my mind. I will clearly get more attention from the ladies if I wear my Michael Jackson outfit. So without further ado, I put on my black leather outfit and white socks.

After putting on my costume, combing my hair, and putting on my stage makeup, I take one last look in the mirror, and just like I have planned, everything looks perfect. One last step and I will be on my way.

I walk out of my bedroom and into the living room to find my parents watching television. Suddenly, my confidence begins to deplete, but I steel my resolve and proceed to ask the most important question of the night.

"Mom, Dad…may I drive your car?"

"What do you need it for, dear?" my mother asks.

I chew the inside of my cheek. "I have a show tonight."

Please don't ask where. Please don't ask where.

If they find out that the show's at Northridge, they'll never let me go. They glance at each other in the way parents always do while they contemplate whether or not to ruin all your plans when a dreaded thought hits me. What if they already know? I mean, it is a public show.

Please don't ask where. Please don't ask where.

"All right," my father says.

"Have fun," my mother replies.

I breathed a sigh of relief, before going over and hugging my dad, then leaning over and giving my mom a kiss on her cheek.

"Thank you, thank you!" I say excitedly. "I'll let you guys know how it goes!"

"Be safe!" Mom says as I pull away.

"Will do!"

Just as I reach for the doorknob, I hear a tune coming from downstairs. Harry. I should probably go say goodbye to him before I head out. Turning around, I head toward the basement and make my way down the stairs. I turn to the right, following the sound of the melody, and I see Harry sitting behind his synthesized piano. I grin as I watch him create a masterpiece right before my very own eyes.

Harry's always been a musical genius, with the dream of releasing music that people would come from all around the world to hear.

All he needs is his big break.

When he presses down on the final keys and lets the sound hang in the air, I applaud, cheering him on as I hope one day thousands of others will do for him too.

Harry jumps, the sounds of my clapping and cheering clearly pulling him out of whatever zone he has just been in.

"You scared me, bro," Harry says.

"Never mind that, what you just played was amazing!"

Harry rubs the back of his neck. "Thanks. I've been up all night working on this." He points a long finger at me, a smirk on his face. "Now I'm going to need you to write the lyrics."

"You got it. I'll start working on it tonight when I get back from the show." I scratch the back of my head. "You sure you don't want to come with me tonight?"

I stand in silence, waiting for his response, hoping he might have changed his mind, but he just drops his head and goes back to composing his song.

"I've still got a lot of work to do," he finally says. "But you'll kill it like always, I know you will. Break a leg out there."

My heart breaks a little inside. It won't be the same without him there. Hiding my disappointment, I stretch out my hand to him. He returns the gesture, and we slap five, snapping fingers as we pull back.

"I'm heading out. Will you be up when I get back?"

"You know I will be."

I give him a half smile. "I'll see you then."

With that, I head out.

When I arrive at the mall, I see the massive, beautiful Northridge Mall perched in the middle of a scenic wonderland. There are man-made lakes all around the facility. Big beautiful trees and bright-green shrubbery line the outside walls. Bustling businesses on every corner.

The parking lot is packed, and hundreds of people are going in and out of the building. There are several businesses that surround Northridge Mall. I see TGI Friday's, Toys "R" Us, and the Northridge Mall Night Club are the most prevalent out of them all. I smile at the sight of the night club, eager knowing in a few hours' time that's where I'll be performing.

I wonder if Lisa'll be there...

I shake the thought out of my head. There's no way she'll come, and even if she will, it doesn't matter. We're done, end of story.

I find a parking spot between the mall and the night-club and make my way over to the shopping center. Who knows, maybe I'll meet a new special someone tonight.

As I make my way up, I see dozens of people staring at me. Most are whispering to one another, and some point at me. I smile at them, the attention revving me up for tonight, and keep walking toward the mall. Before I reach the main entrance, a young boy walks up to me and asks me for my autograph. After signing the little boy's paper, I walked into the mall.

I'm surrounded within minutes. Dozens of people are asking me if I'm Michael Jackson, and though I'll tell them no, they don't care. They still want an autograph and a picture. So I stand in the middle of the mall and start to sign autographs and take pictures. One by one people approach me, and before I realize what is really happening, hundreds of people are surrounding me and congregating in the center of the mall. It comes to a point where security has to get involved. They break up the crowd and start to escort me out of the mall.

Maybe it isn't such a great idea to come to the mall in my costume after all.

Panic starts to rise in my chest. What if Tim thinks I've stood him up? Will he still come to the show? Will anyone from the mall still come to the show after this fiasco?

I see people watching me being escorted out of the mall. Heat rises to my cheeks as embarrassment floods over me. This is not how I envisioned this night starting out. I see people watching me being escorted out of the mall.

I look like I'm getting arrested.

The confidence I had mere minutes ago completely dissipates, and it takes everything in me not to bury my face in my hands.

"We can't wait to see your show tonight!" someone calls out. I look toward them and see a group of girls near the exit I'm heading toward.

"It's pretty cool to have the mall security escorting you around," one of them says. She is gorgeous, with long dark hair and big brown doe-like eyes.

My jaw almost drops.

"Move along," one of the security guards says to them while moving them back.

I make eye contact with the girl one last time and give her a wink as I'm escorted out. My waning confidence suddenly regains by that interaction.

After my "bodyguards" walk me out, I thank them and head for my car. Looks like I am worried for nothing, though I still feel bad about not being able to meet up with Tim. Hopefully he'll come to the show and I can explain everything then.

I make my way toward the nightclub. There's still an hour before it opens, but I figure trying to get in early will be a better option than waiting in my car all that time. Once I make it to the front door, I knock. I wait for a few moments before knocking again when there is no answer.

I look around the near empty parking lot, seeing a few of what must be the workers' cars, when I hear footsteps on the inside.

"We're closed," someone says from the other side of the door. "Come back when we open, and not a minute sooner."

"I'm the Michael Jackson impersonator," I quickly respond. "I'm performing on your main stage tonight. I'd like to survey the location and check the lights and the sound system."

The person on the other end of the door is silent for a few seconds before I hear another set of footsteps nearing the door. I rub my hands together as I hear the two conversing on the inside, before the locks on the door disengage and it's pulled open. Before me stands a good friend. He's a 6-foot-3 Italian bouncer, and he's 250 pounds of pure muscle.

I look up at him and smile. "What's up, Tony?"

"How're you doing?" he says as he opens the door wider. "Come on in."

Tony and I used to work together back in the day and became good friends during that time too. It's good to know that if Tim bails, at least I'll have one familiar face here tonight.

"Man, you won't believe what just happened," I say to him as I enter the club. Tony cocks an eyebrow, signaling me to go on, and I do just that. "I was trying to meet my friend at the food court, and some people stopped to talk to me. No big deal, right? Well, before I knew it, hundreds of people were around me asking for pictures and autographs, and I guess the mall security didn't like it because they forced me to leave."

"No way!" Tony says.

"Yeah, man! They escorted me out of the building and everything like I was a criminal or something. But apparently some people thought they were my bodyguards, shouted they were excited for my show as I left, so I guess it wasn't all bad."

"That's the life of a celebrity for you. Better get used to it."

We both share a laugh before I decide to change the subject.

"So you like working here?"

"It's not so bad," Tony says. "It pays the bills."

"Break up any fights?"

Tony rolls his eyes. "We usually have a good crowd."

I click my tongue. "C'mon, man, don't hold back on me now. I know you have some great stories to tell." I nudged him in the arm. "Just one? For an old friend?"

Tony huffs and shakes his head. "Well, there was this one time…"

"Anthony! Quit your chitchatting and get back to work!" the other guy from before whom I now assume is the manager shouts. "And you, impersonator! Don't you have some lights to check out and a location to survey?"

I scowl at the manager's back as he walks away. He didn't need to be so rude about it.

"I do have a lot of work to do before we open the club," Tony confesses. "Let's reconnect after the show, and I will tell you some of the action I dealt with."

I smile at my friend and give him a fist bump before he goes back to the kitchen and I go toward the stage.

Time passes by in a blur as I methodically check the sound system and the lights to make sure everything will go smoothly during the show. I can't stop thinking about what happened inside the mall. All those people, crowding around *me*. It was overwhelming, yet thrilling. Almost as thrilling as being up on stage.

Almost.

But then the guards had to burst my bubble by basically dragging me out by my leather jacket. As if it was *my* fault. Sure, I may have come dressed up like Jackson, but I wasn't the one that started the scene. That was everyone else's doing for losing their minds. They didn't have to throw me to the curb. But at least some people thought I was still cool. Like that one girl, with the gorgeous long hair, deep brown eyes, and an olive tone skin. The memory of her voice rang in my head—it was rich, lilted, and melodic.

"It's pretty cool to have the mall security escorting you around," she had said.

I hope she comes tonight.

I shake the memory of her and the rest of the previous events away. I can't get distracted. I have a show to do. And it has to be perfect. Especially if she comes.

Focus, J, focus.

I look at the clock on the nearby wall: 6:45 p.m. I need to go backstage before they start letting people in. I don't want anyone to see me before the show starts. Besides, I need to touch up my stage makeup and redo my hair. It needs a little bit more bounce.

I walk toward the back of the club and into the dressing room. There's a table and chair sitting in front of a large mirror with dozens of lights surrounding the frame of the glass. Sitting down in front of it, I open my performance bag and pull out my hair gel, comb, brush, and hair pick. While I'm getting ready, my thoughts wander once again, this time to Tim. I really hope he shows up. I feel so bad. He's probably still sitting there waiting for me. If he doesn't show up, I'll definitely call him after the show or tomorrow at the latest. I want to apologize and explain what happened.

I am pulled from my thoughts when I hear a knock on my door. I look at the clock, and my jaw nearly drops when I see the time: 8:55 p.m. I have been in the dressing room for over two hours. I have been so deep into thought I don't even realize that so much time had passed.

I walk over to the door, and Tony steps into the room.

"It's packed tonight," he says. "Everyone is talking about your show."

My eyes widened. "For real?"

Tony nods. "Knock 'em dead, 'King of Pop.'"

Tony gives me a high five before he turns around and leaves the room, closing the door behind him.

I stand alone in the dressing room. I can feel the sweat already beginning to form on my temple. I reach into my performance bag one final time and pull out my face powder to keep my skin from shining while I'm dancing under the bright lights. When I finish applying it, I look over at the clock: 8:59.

Showtime.

CHAPTER 13

The Pursuit

Jeffrey stands outside the Northridge Mall Nightclub. From what he can see, the inside is jam-packed. He shifts his gaze to the wall and sees a poster hanging similar to the one in his pocket promoting the head performer of the night.

Jerome Turman, the man of the hour.

His man of the hour.

The corner of Jeffrey's lips quirked upward as he stepped forward, opened the door, and entered the club.

CHAPTER 14

Vile Proposition

I hear the MC announcing my name as I stand backstage behind the curtain. I clench and unclench my fingers as I start to feel the adrenaline beginning to flow through my body. The lights go out, and I quickly position myself onstage. The screams and cheers of anticipation get louder and louder the longer the darkness remains, then suddenly, the lights fly back on, the music begins, and I start to dance.

The crowd goes wild. People rush toward the stage and reach for me. I purposefully stay just barely out of their reach as I perform several of Michael Jackson's most popular dance routines to perfection. As I quickly scan the crowd, I look for a familiar face, any familiar face, but everything and everyone just blends together in a sea of heads. Looking away as I turn to the side and strike a pose, I get my head in the game and focus on finishing this thing as flawlessly as I started it.

After fort-five minutes of nonstop dancing, singing, and lip-syncing, the show is coming to a close, and there's only one way to finish this off right: a triple spin and jump in the air and land on my toes in Michael's signature pose. With that, I know I'll have them begging for more. In one fluid motion, I execute the triple spin, leap in the air, and land on my toes as the song finishes. Just like I've practiced dozens of times.

As the palm of my feet land on the floor, my left ankle gives way, caving under the weight of my body with a loud *pop*.

The house lights go dark moments before I collapse onto the ground. I instinctively roll over and reach for my ankle as the crowd continues to cheer. Blinded by the darkness and unaware of my current state of being. At least they don't see my complete blunder.

Forcing myself back to my feet, I limp off the stage before they can turn back on the lights, closing the curtains behind me. As soon as the lights turn back on, I see the face of my best friend Tim waiting for me.

I let out a sharp exhale. "You came."

"I told you I would, didn't I?"

I smile and nod. "Man, I'm really glad to see you." I try to take a step toward him when pain shoots up my leg and I start to collapse.

Tim reaches out and grabs me just before I hit the ground. "Are you all right?"

"I think I broke my ankle on the final pose," I tell him.

"The one you've been practicing for months?"

"The very same."

Tim shakes his head as he slings my arm over his shoulder and helps me to the dressing room.

Tim opens the door and helps me sit down on the chair in front of the vanity mirror. I let out a huge sigh as I lean forward and reach for my ankle. Tim places a hand on my shoulder from behind.

"Let me take a look at it," he suggests.

I glance up at Tim through pain-filled squinted eyes. "What are you going to do, hammer it back into place?"

"What else would you expect?"

We both laugh. The action causes me to grimace as pain shoots back up my ankle.

"For real, though," Tim says, sobering up. "Let me take a look."

Nodding, I take a deep breath and take my shoe and white sock off before rolling up my pants leg, revealing the damage.

"Looks pretty bad, if I do say so myself," Tim says.

I scoff at his diagnosis. "Thank you, Doctor Doom, I can see that for myself."

Tim rolls his eyes. "Whatever. C'mon let me take you to the doctor to get it checked out by a professional."

He tries to help me up, but I pull away with a wave of my finger. "No, sir, we're not going anywhere. We still have some ladies to meet tonight."

Tim raises an eyebrow at me. "You really think you'll be able to enjoy talking to anyone out there while hopping around on a bum leg for the rest of the night?"

"I'll take my chances. We can't let this opportunity slip away, man! Besides, it's starting to feel better."

I start to wiggle it around to prove my point and immediately regret it. Pain shoots up my leg, and I am unable to hide the grimace in my expression from it.

With his arms crossed over his chest, he looks down at the clearly swollen ankle, then back up at my face.

"Could have fooled me."

I rub my face, trying to think up something that would convince Tim that we should stay, when I suddenly remember that I never met up with him at the mall and should just be thankful he's even here to begin with.

I sigh, letting my arms fall limp at my sides. "Hey, man, I want you to know that I didn't mean to stand you up. I was on my way to the food court, but then…"

Tim holds up his hand to stop me midsentence. "I know, I heard what happened. Everyone was talking about it."

I blink back my surprise. "Really?"

Tim nods. "There were a couple of girls that wouldn't shut up about you."

"Did one have really long black hair and big brown doe eyes?"

Tim looks at me with a raised eyebrow. "That's both vague and oddly specific at the same time, but yes, they all did. The group said that they were going to the show tonight. They are probably out there now."

For a moment, the pain in my ankle dissipates as I sit up with great excitement. "Well, what are we waiting for? We have to get out there and find them."

As I move to stand, Tim reaches out his hand to help me, but I stop him.

"I'm good," I say. "I don't want anyone to know that I'm hurt."

"How exactly do you plan to pull that one off?"

"If I can get in there quietly and sit down right away no one will ever know."

Tim dramatically slaps his head. "Why didn't I think of that?"

I roll my eyes and jokingly shove him away. "Go check and see if there's a table with chairs on the edge of the dance floor so we can chill out for the rest of the night, will you?"

"On it."

Tim is only gone for a few minutes before he returns. "I ran into Tony, told him the situation. He's getting someone to set up a table for us."

"Thanks, Tim."

Tim waves off my gratitude. "What are friends for?"

He leans on the wall and looks down at my ankle once again. "How exactly are you planning to have any fun if you can't get onto the dance floor?"

A question I am wondering myself, honestly.

"Hopefully my ankle will start feeling better as the night goes on."

"I wouldn't count on that."

There is a knock on the door.

"Come in," I say.

The door opens, and Tony comes in. "Your table is ready." He looks down at my swollen ankle with a grimace. "You gonna be all right? That looks pretty bad."

I nod my head. "Yeah, I'm fine."

"You should really get that checked out."

"I will tomorrow, but I want to have some fun tonight."

Tony shrugs his shoulders. "Your funeral. If you need anything, you know where to find me."

Tim and I make our way out toward the main area of the club. The strobe lights and music fill my eyes and ears.

Tim points to our table, and I nod my head. It's not that far. A few more feet, and we're home free.

The moment we emerge from out of the hallway, dozens of people rush toward me with big smiles on their faces.

Despite the smile I plaster on my face, I'd be lying if I was ecstatic about this situation. My ankle certainly was not.

Tim quickly steps in between me and the oncoming crowd. "Let's give the man of the hour some space, hm?"

He grabs my shoulder and leads me over to the table, keeping the growing crowd at bay.

Man, I am so thankful he came.

We get to the table, and I plop down on the seat with the most inconspicuous sigh of relief I can muster. Tim puts a hand on my shoulder, and I give him a nod of gratitude.

"You want me to stay here?" Tim asks.

"Nah, man," I say. "Get on out there and find someone to have a good time with."

"If you need anything, just holler."

He and I bump fists, then he turns and disappears into the crowd on the dance floor.

As soon as he's gone, someone else catches my eye. Someone I saw a few hours ago, with long wavy hair, olive skin, and beautiful, big dark-brown doe eyes.

And those doe eyes were currently looking right at me.

The woman from the mall earlier approached. "Mind if I sit here?"

"Not at all," I say, gesturing toward the seat next to me.

She sits down with a smile. "I loved your show," she says. "You did amazing, to no one's surprise."

"All in a day's work."

Her smile brightens, revealing a dimple in the middle of her cheek.

I am completely stunned by her beauty. I can't look away even if I want to, which I most certainly didn't.

Clearing my throat, I gather my composure. "Thank you for coming."

"Do you perform in Milwaukee often?" she asks.

"I live here."

"What a coincidence, so do I." She runs her hand through her hair and tilts her head as she rests her arm on the table. "My name is Kelly."

"Jerome," I reply.

"I know who you are."

She tucks her hair behind her ear, glancing away for a second, before returning her gaze to me. "We should hang out sometime."

I let the corner of my mouth turn up into a half smile. "No time like the present, right?" I hold out my hand to the empty seats surrounding my table. "Care to keep me company for a while?"

I can barely hear anything over the sound of my rapidly beating heart. And the smile she gives me makes it beat harder.

"I'd love to," she says.

I quietly let out a deep breath.

"Let me tell my girlfriends that I'll be joining you for the night." She stands up and takes a few steps backwards, keeping her eyes on me. "Be right back."

With one last dimpled smile, she turns and walks away.

I watch her until she disappears from my view, and even then I don't turn away. I sat there, staring in the direction she went, hoping she really is coming back like she said she would.

I close my eyes and lightly rub my ankle. For a split second I forget about my injury, but that second passes quickly, and the throbbing ache returns to the forefront of my mind.

I hear a chair being pulled out from the table. Someone to help distract me from my ankle. I turned excitedly, hoping it was Kelly, or at least Tim.

It is neither.

In the chair next to me sits a tall, thin, fair-skinned man. His blue eyes are oddly large behind his wide glasses.

"Hello," he says. "I'm Jeff."

"Jerome," I reply.

"I know who you are."

A smile tugs at the corner of his lips as he readjusts himself in his chair.

"I liked your show tonight," Jeff says. "You really do dance and look like the real Michael Jackson."

"Thanks," I say. "I appreciate it. I'm glad you like the show. I hope to see you at the next one."

I glance away from him and back toward the crowd trying to catch a sight of Kelly. I don't want to seem rude to a fan, but I can't help but wonder where she is.

I'm really hoping I haven't been stood up.

Under normal circumstances, I'll be getting up and going to look for her, or even just dancing on the dance floor. But this swollen, throbbing ankle is making sure neither of those things are on the agenda right now.

"I would like to represent you," Jeff says. "Be your agent."

My gaze flickers back to him. Truth be told, I have actually forgotten he is there for that moment. But that request brings my undivided attention back to him.

I tilt my head to the side and raise an eyebrow. "I've had a lot of people at my shows say a lot of things to me, but never that, I will admit." I lean back in my seat. "I already have an agent, though, so thank you for the offer, but I'm going to have to decline."

I begin to turn away, expecting him to leave after my refusal, but instead he stays right where he is, with seemingly no intention of moving.

"I could really help you get your career off the ground."

I shake my head in disapproval. "No thanks."

"Let me help you."

"Sorry, not interested." I turn my head and torso toward the dance floor searching for Kelly.

"Why don't you come by my apartment tonight?" Jeff suggests. "We can have some beers, and I will take some pictures of you."

My complete focus is now back on trying to catch sight of Kelly, my back still toward him. "I'll pass," I say. "Like I said, I've already got someone. Thanks again."

"Don't you want to be a star?"

My eyebrows furrow. His voice suddenly seems a bit more high-pitched than a moment ago, more eager.

"I can make you one," Jeff continues. "Just give me a chance."

I glance back. He's a lot closer than he was before, leaning forward, his arm on the table, eyes intently boring into mine.

"Listen," I say. "I'm flattered by your offers, truly, but the answer is no. Now, I don't mean to be rude, but I'm waiting for someone here and I don't want to miss her. So please excuse me." I turn back around, my back toward him again.

"You're making a big mistake, Jerome."

The chipperness in Jeff's voice is gone, and what remains is a coldness that almost sends chills up my spine.

I see Kelly in the crowd coming toward me.

"Sorry it took me so long," she said. "Me and my girls got into some gossip." She glances over at the man beside me. "Who're you?"

"Jeff," I hear him say behind me.

"You sitting here with us, Jeff?"

"No," I interject a little too forcefully. "No, he was leaving." I dare turn my back to him once more. "Thanks for coming to the show, Jeff."

Jeff's eyes flicker from me to Kelly a few times. His expression is much less inviting than it had been when he first sat down.

"Until next time, then."

CHAPTER 15

Stalking The Prey

"Friend of yours?" Kelly asks as Jeff walks away.

I shake my head. "No, he is not." I look up at her with a grin, changing the subject. "Glad you came back."

"I said I would, didn't I? I am a woman of my word."

Kelly sits down then promptly notices my outstretched leg on the chair beside me. "Are you okay?"

"I'll be fine," I say, rubbing my ankle slightly. "You're very observant."

"Well, I was wondering why you were sitting here all by your lonesome instead of out on the dance floor, but a bum leg is a valid excuse, I suppose."

I chuckle. Kelly has a quick tongue. I like that.

She and I talk back and forth, getting to know each other. I don't even know how much time passes before I hear a group of girls calling out from the dance floor.

"Kelly!" one of the girls says. "Kelly, they're playing your favorite song!"

Just then, Kelly turns to me, and I immediately see the conflicted look in her eye. I give her a warm smirk.

"Go," I say. "I see you want to."

She returns my smirk with a smile of her own. "I'll be back after the song. Don't miss me too much."

With a wink, she stands up and runs to the dance floor.

I close my eyes and listen to the music, moving my head to the beat of the song. Despite the unfortunate circumstances of my leg, the night isn't turning out half bad if I do say so myself.

"Can we take a picture with you?"

I open my eyes to see a couple of people gathered next to my table, one of them holding a camera.

"Of course," I say.

At that moment, my ankle begin to subconsciously throb, but I try to pay it little mind as I carefully stand up from my seat, smile, and strike a pose as they gather around me, and the picture is taken.

The flash from the camera is blinding. I hear them thank me and begin to walk away as I try to blink back my vision. As my eyesight begins to clear a few seconds later, I notice someone else standing in front of me.

Jeff.

"Let me buy you a drink," he says.

He stands there waiting for my response. Motionless. Eyes fixated directly on me. I feel like I'm being scrutinized, examined a little too closely for my liking.

"Thanks for the offer, Jeff," I begin. "But I'm going to pass."

The look on his face after my rejection is not one of disappointment or anger. In fact, I can hardly see any expression at all. He looks…lifeless.

I clear my throat, trying to alleviate the awkwardness that fills the space. "Look, man, do you want an autograph or something?"

"I want to take some pictures of you."

The tone in his voice is almost desperate, it is weird.

I sigh. "All right, fine. Do you have a camera on you?"

"Not here. But my house isn't that far."

I shake my head. "I'm only taking pictures here at the club."

"It's really not that far—"

"I said no!" I say. I can feel my patience wearing thin. "If it's that short of a walk, go get your camera and come back, but I'm not leaving. Pictures are taken here or not at all."

At that moment, Jeff's facial expression changes. No longer is it blank and lifeless. Now it is filled with rage. For a split second, my mind is taken back to the day the taxi driver stalked our house. To the look in my father's eye when I told him no when he tried to hand me the gun.

I eventually did what I was told by my father back then, but this is now, and the man before me isn't my father. So despite the shiver in my spine, I stand my ground.

With arms crossed over my chest, I raise my eyebrows at Jeff, awaiting his response. Clearly not happy with my responses, Jeff pushes his glasses tight on his face then turns and walks away.

I watch him go while rubbing my forehead in frustration.

A hand grasps my shoulder from behind.

I audibly gasp, the volume of the music drowning out the sound.

I leap forward, grabbing the chair in front of me to stop from falling over, before turning around and finding Tim standing behind me, an amused look on his face.

I punch him in the arm. "Man, don't sneak up on me like that!"

"Didn't know you were the type to get easily scared," he says with a smirk.

I plop myself down on the chair. "It's this guy that keeps coming up to me. He's got me on edge."

"That bad, huh?" Tim says, pulling up a chair and sitting on it backward.

"You don't know half of it."

"Can't really complain, though," Tim says. "You did choose this career."

I roll my eyes and groan. "Yeah…true that."

I drop my head and start to rub my temples, trying to combat a headache I can feel coming on. When I look back up, it's not Tim I immediately see. It's Jeff standing in the distance behind him.

"Hey," Tim says. "Earth to J?"

Jeff's watching me, staring directly at me. That blank look still on his face.

"J?"

What is his problem? Why won't he leave me alone?

"J!"

I'm jolted by my best friend's voice once again. My gaze shifts from over his shoulder to him. "Huh?"

"Lost you in la-la land for a second. You good?"

I glance back over his shoulder, but Jeff is gone.

"Yeah," I say, "I'm fine."

I don't particularly feel fine. I feel annoyed, frustrated, and more than a little creeped out. But I can't really see how telling Tim all that would do me any good at the moment.

"Another friend of yours?"

I once again jump at the sudden voice behind me. Turning in my chair, I see Kelly standing next to me. Tim starts laughing.

I glare at Tim, before returning my attention back to Kelly.

"I take it you actually know this guy this time?"

"Unfortunately," I say sarcastically. "Kelly, this is Tim, my best friend. Tim, Kelly."

"A pleasure to meet you, Tim," Kelly says.

"The pleasure is all mine."

I shoot him another glare and mouth "Get your own girl," to which Tim not so subtly rolls his eyes and smirks.

"So," I say, returning my attention to Kelly. "Did you have fun dancing with your girlfriends?"

"Yes, I did. We started a soul train line. Everyone joined in. It was fun."

"That was you who started that?" Tim asks.

Kelly smiles. "Yeah, we did."

"That's so cool," I say. "Whenever I try to start something like that, people just look at me like I'm crazy."

"Because you are crazy," Tim says.

I scoff. "Yeah, for being friends with you."

All three of us share a laugh.

Kelly then says, "Why don't we move this to the bar? I have a friend who's bartending tonight, and since you've introduced me to your best friend, I think it's only fair if I introduce you to one of mine."

"I like that idea." I glance at Tim. "You coming?"

"I could use a drink," Tim says.

"Perfect, you can help me over to the bar."

"That's all I am to you, aren't I? A crutch."

"Absolutely. I'm amazed it took you this long to realize it."

Kelly laughs. She has a beautiful laugh. I think I could listen to it all day.

"You two are hilarious," she says. "I'll meet you by the bar."

As Kelly heads over to the bar, Tim helps me to my feet and slings my arm over his shoulder.

"I better be getting paid for this," he says.

"Don't count on it."

We both give each other bright smiles before we slowly make our way over to the bar.

"So I see you have met the star of the show tonight, Kelly," the bartender says to Kelly as Tim and I approach. Her gaze quickly make its way over me then lingers on Tim. "And I see he brought with him a friend."

Tim struggles for words while his eyes grow wide. I know that look. He is falling, and falling fast.

Kelly turns to me and says, "Jerome, Tim, this is my lifelong friend, Helen."

"A pleasure to meet you," Helen says. Her gaze flickers back to Tim. "Both of you."

Tim suddenly gets cool and collected and gives her a nod. I roll my eyes at him and shake my head. "The pleasure is ours," I say to Helen.

Tim helps me up onto the barstool.

"What happened?" Helen asks as I get situated.

"I blew out my ankle on the last spin I performed just before the lights went dark. Thankfully no one saw as I fell to the floor and practically crawled off the stage."

"You know, I thought I heard a thud after everything went dark."

"Yeah, it's pretty bad. It hurts a lot, but I'll be okay."

"Good to hear. So!" Helen clasps her hands together. "What're we all drinking tonight?"

"I'll have my usual," Kelly says.

Helen nods and looks at me.

"Just a glass of water, please."

"Simple, makes my job easier." Helen turns to Tim. "And for you, pretty boy?"

Even with the club's dim lights, I'm sure I see a hint of red crawl up Tim's cheeks.

"I'll take whatever you suggest."

A grin forms on Helen's face. "Coming right up."

The four of us all chatted together for some time, Helen stepping away from time to time to help a customer, but as the night went on, Helen and Tim move to the other end of the bar, leaving me and Kelly to our own devices.

"So tell me about yourself," I say. "What do you do for a living?"

"Well, I'm currently a freshman at Marquette," Kelly replies. "I'm studying to be a nurse."

"A respectable profession."

"I'll say." Kelly takes a sip of her drink. "And you? Is this what you've always wanted to do?"

"What can I say? I love to perform," I confess.

Kelly smiles. "I can definitely tell." She sets her empty glass down on the counter. "I should probably go check on my other friends. It's been awhile."

I try to hide the disappointment I feel, but I can tell Kelly notices with the smirk she gives me.

"Don't worry, sad eyes, I'll be right back. I won't leave you alone too long with those two lovebirds."

I glance over at Tim and Helen, and lo and behold, they do seem quite oblivious to the rest of the world.

"How'd you know they'd hit it off?" I ask.

Kelly shrugs. "I know Helen like the back of my hand. And even from such a short time knowing Tim, I knew right away that he was her type." She rests her hand on my shoulder as she stands up from the bar. "I'll be right back."

I watch her go like I do every time. My hand rests on the place where her hand has just been.

This night keeps getting better and better.

CHAPTER 16

Trapped In A Cell

I grab the pitcher of water Helen left me on the counter to refill my glass. As I take a sip, I glance up into the large mirror mounted on the wall behind the bar and see Jeff standing directly behind me.

"What happened to your leg?" he asks me once I notice him.

This is starting to get ridiculous. He just keeps showing up out of nowhere.

"Nothing," I say as I set down my glass. "Just a little accident at the end of the show."

He hums as if he was mulling over my words.

I turn to face the man who's gotten quite recognizable tonight.

"You should really let me be your agent," Jeff says.

It takes everything in me to not roll my eyes. He really won't let this go.

"Listen, Jeff, I've said it before, and I'm not changing my answer. I already have an agent, and I am very happy with his work."

"If you just let me take some pictures of you, I could make you a star."

Okay, this is getting ridiculous. My current agent has never asked to take pictures of me, and if he wants some photos, he will send me to a modeling agency to have them done professionally.

What does this guy want from me? Why can't he take no for an answer? I am never going anywhere with this guy, and I can't understand how he can't see that. I push myself up from the chair and stand to face him, supporting myself with the back of the stool.

"Look, man, I am sure there are a lot of people who would love to have you as their agent, but I already have representation and I am happy with everything they do for me. So as much as I appreciate your interest, I must politely decline your proposition. But thank you for the offer."

At that very moment, his facial expression changes like last time. It becomes stoic and cold, and that chill goes down my spine once more.

"Okay," Jeff says, then turns around and walks away. Just like that.

Slowly I lower myself down on the stool at the bar. I grab my water and take a big gulp. A few minutes later, Kelly comes bounding back to me, a bright smile on her face. "I'm back."

Her smile fades as she gets a good look at me. "Jerome? You okay?"

I shook my head. "It's nothing. Just…Jeff."

"The guy from before?" Kelly asks as she sits down on the stool next to mine. "He came back over to you?"

I nod my head, exasperated. "Tried to get me to go over to his house and wouldn't take no for an answer."

"What if I do the same thing?" Kelly asks, a smirk tugging at her lips. "You gonna reject me too?"

I raise an eyebrow and give her a half grin. "Ask me and find out."

"I'll think about it."

She's playing hard to get, I see. Well, two can play at that game.

She and I continue our conversation and banter until I'm subsequently reminded of how much water I have been drinking.

"I have to take a quick trip to the restroom," I say, pushing myself off my seat. "I'll be back in a sec—"

Pain shoots up my ankle as I proceed to put most of my weight on it the moment I hop down from the seat. I have completely forgotten about my busted ankle. If it's my luck, I probably just busted it more.

Kelly gets up from her own seat, wraps one arm around me, and presses her other hand on my chest to help stabilize me.

"Easy there," she says. "You might need some help."

She looks up at me then over my shoulder. "Tim!" she shouts.

Tim, who doesn't look like he's moved since he started talking to Helen, looks over in our direction.

"Mind giving your best friend a hand? He needs to go to the little boys' room."

"Hey!" I say to her.

She gives me a jovial smile while Tim and Helen both make their way over to us.

"Don't you boys take too long now," Helen says, resting her arms on the bar top. "We'll be waiting."

The girls laugh with each other while Tim grabs me from under my arms and helps me to the bathroom.

"I got it from here," I say to Tim as we enter the bathroom. I try to hop over to the urinal, but I am unable to stand and support myself.

Tim stands there with his arms crossed. "Are you sure you don't need my help?"

"I'm sure. I'll just use the stall."

"You do that. I'll be outside."

Tim leaves, and I'm left alone. I hop over to the first stall and sit down, reaching forward to lock the door behind me.

While leaning against the wall outside the bathroom, Tim sees Kelly approaching.

"I'll help him back to the bar when he comes out," Kelly says. "Besides, I need to freshen up in the ladies' room right next door."

"Cool. Let me tell J." Tim opens the bathroom door and yells inside, "Kelly's here, and she'll help you back to the bar after she fixes her makeup in the girls' bathroom."

Kelly slaps Tim across the arm. Tim laughs and walks away. Kelly goes into the ladies' room.

A few moments later, while sitting in the bathroom stall, I hear someone enter the bathroom. He stops for a moment and then starts walking again. It sounds like he is pacing. The sound of his footsteps fade as he seems to walk toward the opposite end of the bathroom, then those same footsteps get louder once more as he walks back toward my stall. The sound of his steps seems slow and deliberate. As he nears my stall, I expect him to walk past and continue pacing back and forth, but he doesn't. When he reaches my stall, he comes to a complete stop and faces my stall and stands there perfectly still. He is so close that I try to make out the person through the crack of the stall, but I don't need to. I know who it is standing outside my door.

It's him.

It's Jeff. He's followed me into the bathroom, and now he's standing in front of my bathroom stall. I look up to make sure I latched the bolt. It's locked, but I still don't feel secure. I slowly pull up my pants, bracing myself for his entry. I tell myself, *If he comes in here, he's in for the fight of his life.* But the reality is, I can't fight at all because I have no balance and I'm in great pain.

What if he has a knife? I am a dead man if he comes through that door. I can't even run. So all I can do is wait and hope that he will just walk away. However, after several, long minutes he's still standing in front of my stall. I try to reason with him and say, "This stall is taken. Why don't you try another one." I wait for a reply. There is nothing but silence. It feels like hours have passed and he's still standing outside my door. My legs are starting to go numb from sitting on the toilet for so long. My heart starts racing, and my mind starts looking for a way out. I turn to the only source that has never failed me. A source that I always gravitate to in times of trouble. I begin to silently pray.

Father in heaven, rescue me from this devilish adversary in human form. Protect me from all that is evil. I have done nothing to offend this man, and yet he won't go away. What should I do?

Suddenly the sound of humming pierces the air, reaches my ears, and penetrates my soul. I quickly realize it's coming from him as he continues to stand motionless in front of my stall. Several more minutes go by. It feels like a lifetime.

Lord, please, don't stay silent. Listen to my cry for help and lift Your holy hands and unleash thy judgment against this wicked assailant outside my door. Fight against this man who spoke friendly words to me while planning evil in his heart. Deal with me generously, so that I may survive and glorify your name.

I shiver and quake in fear. The dread that overwhelms my soul pours through my spirit with trembling trepidation. My breath is short, and my lips are parched. I am frozen with horror, trapped in a stall with no escape. I begin to sweat profusely. I start wringing my hands. I can feel the perspiration forming between my fingers. Is this it? Is he going to attack? Has God turned his ears away from my cries? Have I angered Him? Is His wrath now being unleashed against me? I start to tremble in fear because for the first time in my life I feel alone, trapped in a bathroom stall with the devil outside my door.

I know I don't deserve your help, but I now beg for your forgiveness and your mercy. Deliver me, Lord, that I may live. Stretch forth your mighty arm and provide for me a way out of this. I cry out for your deliverance. Save me. O God above, please save me. In the name of Jesus, I beg of you to answer my prayer.

Just when I think all hope is gone and Jeff is going to burst into my stall, he stops humming, then turns and walks away. I take a deep breath and slowly stand up. I am bracing myself on the side wall of the stall. I wait a few minutes to listen for sounds in the bathroom. I don't hear anything. There's no movement at all. So I slowly unlatched the door and peeked out from behind the door. I surveyed the room. It's completely empty. I think he's gone. I exit the stall and slowly start to limp toward the exit door. My heart is pounding with great intensity. My head is on a swivel. I am looking to my left and my right. I am constantly looking behind me. I don't see anyone.

It feels like hours, but I finally reach the door and push it open. I hesitate before stepping out of the bathroom and into the hallway. After a few seconds, I look down the hall. I look both ways. It's dark, but I can see that the hallway is empty. No one is in sight, and Kelly is still in the ladies' room. I lean against the wall. I am staring down the hallway waiting for Jeff to appear. It takes a few minutes before Kelly comes out of the bathroom. She smiles and gives me her shoulder to lean on. I put my arm around her and prepare to limp down the hall. I take one last look at the now-closed men's bathroom door then turn away as I try to forget what just occurred.

We start walking down the hall. I contemplate the idea of telling Kelly what happened, but I talk myself out of it. I don't want her to think that I am not man enough to handle a deranged fan. She might not ever feel safe around me. If I can't protect myself, how could I ever protect her? So I keep quiet.

Before we reach the end of the hall, I can't fight the urge to take one final look at the men's bathroom. So I look back, and to my horror, the men's bathroom door is now wide open. I am stunned by what I see. I can't believe it. How could that be? While I am still trying to understand what happened, we reach the bar. However, my eyes are still fixed on the men's bathroom door. Kelly helps me sit down, but I'm still looking down the hallway. I am scanning the long, dark hallway. It's totally empty. There's no one in sight. All I see is a dark hallway and the one open door with the white light flooding out of the men's bathroom. I start to analyze and ponder the situation. *How could the door be open? Did I forget to close it? No one passed us on the way out, and no one has entered the hallway since we sat down. It doesn't make sense. Maybe the door works on sensors? But why is it still open? Is someone still standing inside the bathroom doorway and keeping the door open? No way! I looked around the entire bathroom. There was no one in there when I left. Unless he was in another stall? Nope! I would have seen him walk past me again.*

After several minutes of being lost in my thoughts, Kelly taps me on the shoulder and says, "Hello! Are you still with me?"

I snap out of it, turn toward her, and say, "I'm sorry. I'm just a little distracted right now. Let's get back to us." She smiles and picks up the conversation right where she left off before we took a stroll to the restrooms. She's a talker, and that's a good thing because my mind is somewhere else. I'm still rehearsing the bathroom incident in my mind. I repeatedly go over every aspect of that latest encounter with Jeff. I ask myself, *Was there anything that I could've done differently? Should I have called for help?* I quickly dismiss that last thought because I believe that if I have called out, Kelly will have lost all respect for me.

Poor Kelly, she's just chatting away. I am looking at her, but I don't hear anything she's saying. I try to let the incident go and focus on Kelly, but I find myself looking around the club trying to spot Jeff. I don't see him anywhere. Maybe he left. I hope so. He's ruining my night.

Kelly finally notices that I am ignoring her and says, "Well, since you're not listening to me, I think I am going to check in with my girls."

I try to apologize. "I'm sorry. Please forgive me. Don't go. You've got my undivided attention."

She responds, "It's okay. I understand. You are a popular guy, and you have a lot of fans that need your attention. I get it. I'm not upset. I just need to keep my friends happy too. They worry about me." She smiles. "I'll be right back." She stands up and walks away.

I almost feel relieved. I can now focus on the problem at hand. Where's Jeff?

I scan the club, but I don't see him. I look down the hallway to see if he's near the bathroom. I notice that the men's bathroom door is now closed. It's been almost an hour since the incident occurred, so that doesn't surprise me. So I continue to look around the nightclub, but there is no sight of my stalker.

I decided to shift gears and start looking for Tim. I want to tell him what happened. I check the dance floor, but he's not there. After scanning most of the nightclub, I say to myself, *Maybe Tim's sitting at our table? He's probably tired from dancing all night.* So I turn to look at our private corner of the club, and sitting in the middle of my table is a drink. I look around the area to see if Tim is near. *Maybe it's his drink?* I don't see Tim anywhere.

I turn back to the bar and look for Helen. She's handing someone a drink. I get her attention, and she walks over. I ask her a question. "Hey, Helen. Why is there a drink on my table? I didn't order it."

Helen says, "Your friend bought you a drink."

I look stunned and say, "What friend?'

She says, "The guy you were talking to about an hour ago."

I realize she must have seen the conversation I had with Jeff at the bar.

I replied, "He's not my friend. He's just some crazy fan who won't take no for an answer."

"I'm sorry. I didn't know. What do you want me to do with it?"

"Throw it out. I don't want it."

"Okay." She walks from behind the bar, over to my table, picks up the glass, walks back to the bar, and tosses it out.

I look at her and say, "Thanks. What was it?"

"Beer."

I am now sick to my stomach. That's what he has been pitching to me all night. I know it was him. I wonder, *Is he trying to send me a message? He wants me to know that he sent the drink. This guy is relentless. I think he wants more than just a working relationship. He wants me!*

I know he's watching me. I wish Kelly was here. I could cuddle close to her so he can see that I am with someone and that I have zero interest in him and his so-called talent agency.

Just then Kelly walks up. I look at her and say, "Boy, are you a sight for sore eyes."

She replies, "I have some bad news. My friends are ready to leave."

I look crushed and say, "Are you leaving with them?"

She says, "We all came here together. I need them to take me home."

A smile comes over my face and hope fills my heart. I have only one question to ask. "Would you like for me to take you home?"

She hesitates, looks me in the eyes, and says, "I would like that, but my friends will want to meet you before they leave."

I respond, "Of course. Bring them over. I would like to meet them too."

She smiles and says, "Okay. I'll go get them."

I reply, "Can you help me over to my table before you leave? I don't want them to think that I'm hanging out at the bar."

She laughs and says, "Sure." Kelly helps me off the stool and supports me as we walk over to the table. I sit down, and she says, "I'll be right back." She walks away.

I start to look around the club for Tim. I can't find him anywhere. He must have left with someone. Well, at least he's having fun tonight. I start looking around the room for Jeff. I know he's still watching me. I'm going to get real close to Kelly, maybe hold her hand the rest of the night so he can see that I'm with someone. Maybe he'll leave me alone.

I see Kelly and her five friends walking toward me. I smile and wave as they approach. Kelly introduces them to me. "Jerome, these are my friends. This is Diane, Janet, Maria, Shelly, and Felisha."

"It's a pleasure to meet all of you," I say.

"It's nice to meet you too," Diane says. "I loved your show."

"Thank you. I appreciate all of you for coming out to see me perform tonight."

"I came out to party. I didn't even know you were per-forming tonight," Felisha admits.

We all laugh.

"But I did enjoy your show," she continues.

"Thank you." I look at the group of girls and say, "So all of you fit in one car?"

Maria says, "I know it's too crowded. I'm so glad Kelly is riding home with you. Now, I don't have to sit on some-one's lap on the way home."

"You better take care of our girl. Get her home safe."

"I will."

"Have you been drinking?" Maria asks me.

"I don't drink."

"Good."

"Are you high?" Felisha asks.

"I don't take drugs."

"Do you have any brothers?" Janet asks.

Felisha hits her friend's arm. "Shut up, Janet!"

"I'm serious!"

I chuckle. "Yes, but they don't live here. They live in California."

"I don't care," Janet says "I'll move." The other girls roll their eyes. Janet scoffs at her friends. "What's with the attitude? I'm trying to meet me a Michael Jackson too."

Kelly puts her hand on her hip and says, "His name is Jerome Turman. He's not a Jackson."

"Well, he looks like one, and I want one too."

"I will let my brothers know that you would like to meet them," I chime in.

"Thank you."

"You are so embarrassing," Diane says. "Let's go, ladies."

They all hug Kelly and wave goodbye to me and start to walk away.

Kelly turns and looks at me and says, "I think I left my bag in the car. I need to get it before they leave."

I say, "Okay."

She turns and starts to walk toward them. She calls out to them, "Hey, wait up. I'm going to walk you to the car."

I watch them walk to the front of the club and open the exit door. As the door swings open, I see someone. I see Jeff standing outside the front door looking into the nightclub. The door slowly closes, and Jeff stands motionless and continues to peer inside.

I immediately begin to worry about Kelly. I try to stand up and limp over to the front door, but by the time I get halfway there, Kelly walks back into the club. I stop and take a deep breath. I feel totally relieved that she's all right. But now my concern has turned to complete frustration and anger.

She walks up to me and says, "Why are you up? Where are you going?"

"Let's get out of here."

She looks shocked. "You want to leave?"

"Yeah, let's go somewhere where everybody doesn't know us. I feel like a fish in an aquarium."

"Okay. But I want to say goodbye to Helen." I agree. She helps walk me back to the bar. Kelly helps me sit down, walks over to Helen, and says, "Hey, girl, I'm heading out. We need to keep in touch."

Helen says, "I know. I miss my girl. We should all hang out sometimes. I would love for you to meet my friend Richie."

Kelly says, "Ooooh, girl, tell me all about him, but what happened to Tim?"

Kelly shakes her head in disappointment and starts to talk about Richie.

I sigh. This is going to take a while. I might as well sit back and try to relax. But that's not going to happen until I can get out of this club and get away from Jeff.

I can hear Kelly and Helen talking about everything under the sun. I am still looking around. I don't see anyone I recognize. I look on the dance floor hoping to see Tim, but he's not there. It's just me and Kelly here now, and it's not good that I am sitting here alone with my thoughts. I start to reflect on everything that has happened tonight. I am still shaken by the incident in the bathroom. I don't think I'll ever get over that.

The way he looked at me throughout the night was so menacing. I felt like he was a hunter and I was his prey. No one has ever looked at me like that before. I can still feel his eyes piercing into my soul.

I can't believe he would get so angry just because I rejected his proposal. He actually wanted to fight me over that. I guess some people just can't take no for an answer. I take one last look around the nightclub. I don't see Jeff. I think he's gone. I guess he never came back inside. I start to feel relieved, but I still want to leave. I want to get this night over with.

I see Kelly exchanging phone numbers with Helen. Kelly walks over to me and says, "Okay, I'm ready to go."

I wave goodbye to Helen. Kelly helps walk me over to the front door. A few patrons say goodbye and wished me the best as I limp toward the exit. I thank them for coming to the show and continue to make my way to the door.

When I reach the exit, I look out the side window, and I see a dark, shadowy figure standing between the exit door and the parking lot. The silhouette looks like a tall thin man. He's just standing in the dark, motionless and facing the building. It looks like he's just waiting for someone to exit. Could that be Jeff, or am I just paranoid? Well, I don't want to find out. So I turn toward Kelly and say, "Hey, I want to say goodbye to my friend that I came here with.

Can we head back toward the dance floor for a few minutes? I want to see if I can find him."

Kelly says, "Sure. No problem." She helps me walk back toward the dance floor.

We stop at the edge of the dance floor, and I proceed to search the area. I am desperately hoping that I see Tim, but he's nowhere to be found.

Kelly says, "Do you see him?"

"No. He must have left." I continue to look around the room. Suddenly I see Jeff standing inside the nightclub. He's lurking in the corner by the front door. He's looking directly at me. My heart starts to rapidly pound in my chest. My sweat glands open up. For the first time tonight, I am terrified. He's not going away. He's watching everything I do and everywhere I go. This is going to end badly. I am going to have to deal with this guy. But how? I can't fight him with a broken ankle. He won't listen to reason. If I try to leave, he's just going to follow me. I can't let this guy know where I live. I can't have another psycho come to our house.

Just then it hits me. I suddenly remember what my father told me: "Let this be a lesson to all of you. In stressful times, never panic. Stay focused and clear minded. Always be prepared. Have a plan of action. Try to think two or three steps ahead of your adversary and don't be afraid to act. This may save your life one day."

I take a deep breath and my heart slows to a normal pace. I then say to myself, *That's it! I'm tired of being a victim. It's time to pull out the big guns.*

"Where's Tony?" I start looking around for my good friend Tony. I don't see him anywhere. However, I know he's still here. I just have to find him. I ask Kelly to help me look in the back for my friend. She assists me. We search the kitchen and the dressing room. I can't find him, but I will not stop until I do.

Eventually, I see Tony standing by the DJ booth, and my eyes light up. I say to Kelly, "There he is! Can you help me over to the DJ booth?"

She nods her head in approval. I walk up to Tony and say, "Man, you gotta help me!"

"What's wrong?" he asks.

"That guy standing in the corner has been stalking me all night. He won't leave me alone. I don't think he has good intentions. He's a threat, and I don't feel safe at all. I believe he would even follow me home."

Tony's facial expression changes. A look of determination and sheer willpower illuminates his face. I can actually see his massive muscles flexing from underneath his uniform. He fixes his eyes on Jeff and says, "J, you have nothing to worry about. This guy won't be a problem anymore tonight. I got you."

Tony walks away from the DJ booth and toward Jeff. He starts to ask Jeff some questions. I can't hear what they are saying, but I can tell that Tony is clearly not happy with Jeff's answers. He points to the exit door, but Jeff refuses to leave. Tony grabs Jeff's arm and escorts him outside. I watch the exit door and wait for Tony to walk back into the club.

Kelly looks at me and says, "What's going on?"

"It's okay," I responded. "I'm handling it."

Kelly looks confused and says, "Handling what?"

I say, "It's just an unruly fan. This happens sometimes."

I don't want to tell her the full story. It's too embarrassing. I feel so helpless, and I don't want her to know that.

Several minutes go by before Tony comes back into the club. He walks over to the DJ booth and says, "It's taken care of."

"What happened?" I ask.

"I handled it."

"Is it safe to leave?"

"You have nothing to worry about."

"Are you sure?"

"Trust me," Tony says. "You will never be bothered by him again."

I take a deep breath and put my free hand on Tony's shoulder and said, "Thank you so much."

"No problem."

As Kelly and I leave, I start to think to myself, *What did Tony do? How can he be so sure that it's safe?* I carefully scan the room looking for Jeff. He's nowhere to be found. He definitely hasn't come back inside the club. We work our way closer to the exit door. I stop and look out the side window. The parking lot is clear. No one is outside. The coast is clear.

We walk out the front door and slowly start walking toward my car. I am looking everywhere for Jeff. I am constantly looking behind me and scanning the area around every car we pass. We are getting closer to my car. I have to make sure no one is following me. I continue to look behind me. I am extremely paranoid. I know that Kelly can tell that I am worried, but she stays silent. She seems so brave. I feel like such a wimp, but I have to remind myself that she has no clue what all happened tonight, and it's going to stay that way.

We finally reach my car. I begin to worry about the rumors of someone hiding under the car. What if Jeff is hiding under my car? He could cut my ankle, and I would be helpless to stop him. I then say to myself, *Stop it! He's not hiding under my car. How would he even know what my car looks like?*

Kelly holds me up while I reach for my keys. She says, "How are you going to drive?"

I responded, "It's my left ankle. I can use my right foot for the gas and brake pedals." I put the keys in the lock and take one last look around the area. The parking lot is completely empty. There is no one outside. I can only see cars parked outside the nightclub. The shopping mall closed hours ago. I am about to open the door and get inside the car, but I hesitate and slightly open the driver-side door just enough to trigger the inside dome lights. I need to see that no one is waiting to attack me inside the car.

After the lights come on, I can see that the car is empty. Kelly helps me get inside. She walks around to the passenger side and gets in the car. I start the engine, put the car in gear, and drive off.

Kelly and I don't even say one word to each other during the entire trip to her house. There is dead silence throughout the ride. We don't even turn on the radio. The whole time I repeatedly look in the rearview mirror to see if anyone is following us. I diligently watch every car that follows behind me until they turn off the road or go in another direction. I look into the face of every man walking down the road or standing on the street corner.

Once I get her home, I thank her for a good night. She smiles, opens the car door, steps out of the car, and goes inside.

That is the last time I will ever see Kelly. We don't exchange phone numbers, and we don't even talk about seeing or talking to each other ever again after the final incident at the club.

As I'm about to make my way home, I check the rear-view mirror to see if anyone is watching. I don't see anyone. I carefully look both ways before I leave her house. I desperately need to make sure no one has followed us. I don't see any cars on the street that night. I put the car in reverse and slowly back out of the driveway. After reaching the street, I put the car in gear and drive home. It takes me an hour. Not because of the distance between our two houses, but because I deliberately keep rerouting my path in order to elude anyone who may be following me. After dozens of unnecessary right turns, I finally make it home.

I am totally convinced that no one followed me. I made so many turns that I almost got lost. No one could have followed me home that night. I struggle to exit the car. My ankle is really sore after putting so much weight on it throughout the night.

After getting out of the car and locking the doors, I start to limp around the front of the car when I see a car approaching. Its headlights appear to be heading straight toward me. I freeze and stand paralyzed in fear. I am maintaining my balance by leaning on the hood of the car. I think about running, but I know that's not a real option. I consider ducking down behind the car, but I can't do that either. How will I get back up? So I just stand there and watch. The car gets closer and closer to my house. I am like a deer looking into the headlights of an oncoming vehicle. I brace myself for what's about to happen. But to my relief, the car just drives by.

I still can't feel any relief because I wonder if that was Jeff. He might know where I live now. This is a nightmare.

I am tense until I see the car pull into my neighbor's driveway. I watch until he gets out of his car, walks up to his front door, pulls out his keys, and walks into his house. I am relieved that it is not Jeff. I gather myself and continue limping back toward my house. I am checking all around the outside of my house. I am looking up and down the street to make sure no one is watching. After finally reaching the front door, I unlock it and enter the house.

I take one final look outside. There is no one around. The night is finally over. I close the door and lock every latch available.

After several trips to the front door to check outside, it takes me hours to calm down before I can fall asleep. Needless to say, it is a restless night. Until I remember what God has done for me that night. I decide to go to Him with a prayer of thanksgiving, "Oh merciful, kind, and gracious Heavenly Father, I praise Your holy name for You heard my cry. I prayed and You answered me. You freed me from all my fears. In my time of desperation, I prayed unto You, and You listened to me. You defended me and removed the threat that was before me. I trusted in You with all my heart, and You helped me, and my soul is now filled with peace and joy. You are my strength, my shield, and my salvation. I will burst out in songs of thanksgiving and make a joyful noise unto Lord for You have wrapped Your arms around me and carried me close to Your heart forevermore. For thine is the kingdom and the power forever and ever. In the name of Jesus, I pray, amen!"

After I finish praying, I close my eyes and sleep peacefully for the rest of the night.

Little do I know that I have escaped the clutches of a serial killer that night. What I do know is that horrific experience will change me for the rest of my life.

CHAPTER 17

The Beast Revealed

I was a trusting, open, free-spirited young man, without a care in the world. But after that night, I become paranoid, isolated, ever vigilant, watching everyone, barely able to sleep at night, always locking my doors, keeping my windows shut and the blinds closed tight. I start training and practicing martial arts. I am preparing for an intruder or another encounter with evil, and if I'm away from home, I'm always looking to identify every exit at all locations both public and private. I become a perfect candidate for psychological therapy, but instead of seeing a doctor, I decide to try and bury the memory of that night at the club and put it in the past. And I do just that. It stays hidden in my mind until one day the news breaks about a recently arrested serial killer who hunted his prey on the streets of Milwaukee. The news is being aired on every channel. It is a horrific story of deception, murder, and cannibalism. I feel sick to my stomach whenever I think about those poor victims and their families.

It isn't until the next day, however, that they release the name and the image of the murderer to the public. And when they do, I can't believe my eyes.

My hands shake as I hold the morning newspaper in my hand, the terror of that repressed night instantly flooding back as I stare at the image of Jeff on the front page.

I collapse into the living room sofa and begin to read the article. I learn that his full name is Jeffrey Dahmer. I read about the atrocities he committed on his victims. How he targeted people of color. But the most terrifying information is the method he used to deceive his victims into his house of death. He would tell his victims that he wanted to take pictures of them and drink some beers. He conned them into coming over to his house and murdered them. That was my fate that night. He had marked me for death. I thought to myself, *God was watching over me that night, and He delivered me from evil. I am so thankful to be alive. That could have been me. They could have found my remains in his apartment. But I escaped. I survived a brush with death. I stared into the face of evil and lived.*

Just then the phone rings. I get up and walk over to the phone, pick up the receiver, and place it to my ear and say, "Hello."

I hear Tim's voice on the other line. He says, "Hey, J, did you see today's newspaper?"

I say, "Yeah, I'm reading it right now."

Tim then says, "Did you see the story about the guy who was killing and eating people? Man, that's the guy who was stalking you at Northridge last year!"

I am stunned. Tim recognizes him too. I don't have to prod him into trying to remember the incident or what Jeff looks like. As a matter of fact, I don't even bring up the subject. He calls me, and he thinks he is telling me that Jeffrey Dahmer is my stalker. There is no doubt in my mind. This conversation confirms it. But I don't need Tim to tell me that Jeff's picture is on the front page of the newspaper. I know it is him. I will never forget the face of the man who stalked me. It was Jeffrey Dahmer that terrorized me that night at the Northridge Mall.

CHAPTER 18

A Damaged Soul

Several years have passed, and Jeffrey Dahmer has been convicted of murder and is serving his life sentence at the Columbia Correctional Institute in Portage Wisconsin.[14] On November 28, 1994, Jeffrey Dahmer and his fellow inmate, the infamous Jesse Anderson, are assigned to clean the prison gym. Around 8:10 a.m., inmate Christopher Scarver,[15] who is also designated to clean the gym that morning, corners Jeffrey in the bathroom. Scarver pulls out a newspaper clipping from his pocket and confronts Jeffrey about the details of his crimes. Scarver then violently attacks Jeffrey in the bathroom. With fierce disgust over the murders, Scarver lashes out and severely bludgeons Jeffrey with an iron bar he has concealed in his clothing. Jeffrey receives numerous blows to the head and face area during the attack.

---

[14] "Jeffrey Dahmer." 2023. Wikipedia. September 19, 2023. https://en.wikipedia. org/wiki/Jeffrey_Dahmer#:~:text=On%20November%2028%2C%20 1994%2C%20Dahmer.

[15] Goldfarb, Kara. 2018. "Meet Christopher Scarver — the Man Who Killed Cannibal Jeffrey Dahmer." All That's Interesting. All That's Interesting. March 15, 2018. https://allthatsinteresting.com/christopher-scarver-jeffrey-dahmer-death.

Scarver also smashes Jeffrey's head repeatedly against the bathroom wall. While Jeffrey lies dying on the bathroom floor, Scarver proceeds to track down Jesse Anderson. After finding him, Scarver uses the same iron bar to inflict massive wounds to Anderson's head. While Jeffrey and Anderson lie motionless on the bathroom floor, Scarver walks back to his cell and waits for the guards to arrive. When the guards question him about leaving his work detail early, Scarver admitted to the murders. Jeffrey and Anderson are found lying in a pool of blood. They will both eventually die from their wounds. Two men forever linked together in death have another connection. One that only those who lived that fateful night with me know about. The ties that bind two killers to one infamous location. The link between life and death, murder and survival. The connection is that place that is now abandoned. A place that will forever be remembered as the Ghost Mall. Where lives have been lost and changed forever. It's the place known as the Northridge Mall. Its memory has scarred me for life.

My fear of public places resonates to this day. When I walk out the door of my home, I am on constant alert, always aware of my surroundings. I question the people that I see, even those who may be completely harmless. Are they safe to be around? I know everyone can't be bad. However, my mind is trapped with these thoughts that I cannot overcome. Sometimes I must gather the courage to just walk outside knowing that death may be lurking in the shadows. Even when I go grocery shopping, I will walk out of the store if I see a suspicious person, leaving my groceries behind and accepting the fact that I will have to shop another day.

When I go to church on a Sunday morning, if a stranger visits the assembly, I will walk out or move close to an exit so I can leave unscathed in case of an incident. I live in fear all because of this Milwaukee Monster. My lack of trust toward strangers takes me back to that night. The reality that I had become the next target for the man known as the Milwaukee Cannibal will haunt me for the rest of my life.

I never perform again. Northridge was the last time I impersonated Michael Jackson. I eventually go back to school and major in broadcasting. I have many adventures during my time as a television news anchor. I am taken hostage once and receive numerous death threats. I will even meet the future president of the United States of America, Bill Clinton. But that's a story for another time.

If you think this is a happy ending, you will be wrong. My life has been a nightmarish existence since that fateful encounter with a serial killer. However, my complete story has not yet been told. The final chapter has not yet been written. The best is yet to come.

About the Author

Jerome Turman

Nancy Treskow

Celina Turman

Jerome Turman worked for fifteen years as a television news anchor for the NBC affiliate TMJ-4 in Milwaukee, the FOX affiliate FOX-47 in Madison, and the ABC affiliate ABC-27 in Madison. Turman wrote, produced, and reported hundreds of stories that were broadcasted live on air over those years.

Jerome is also a storyteller at heart. He has written several screenplays and TV shows for his movie production company. He co-owns D'Turman Productions, a movie and television production company, also located in Milwaukee, Wisconsin. His work can be found at dturmanproductions.com and the D'Turman TNT Network on Roku and YouTube streaming services.

www.ingramcontent.com/pod-product-compliance
Lightning Source LLC
Chambersburg PA
CBHW022017150726
47990CB00002B/703